FISHBOURNE
ROMAN PALACE

FISHBOURNE
ROMAN PALACE

Barry Cunliffe

TEMPUS

Revised and updated edition first published 1998
Reprinted 1999

Published by:
Tempus Publishing Limited
The Mill, Brimscombe Port
Stroud, Gloucestershire, GL5 2QG

© Barry Cunliffe, 1971, 1998

The right of Barry Cunliffe to be identified as the Author of this work has been asserted by him in accordance with the Copyrights, Designs and Patents Act 1988.

Typesetting and origination by Tempus Publishing Ltd.
Printed and bound inGreat Britain.

All rights reserved. No part of this book may be reprinted or reproduced or utilised in any form or by any electronic, mechanical or other means, now known or hereafter invented, including photocopying and recording, or in any information storage or retrieval system, without the permission in writing from the Publishers.

British Library Cataloguing in Publication Data.
A catalogue record for this book is available from the British Library.

ISBN 07524 1408 9

Contents

List of illustrations		6
Preface		9
1	Discovery	11
2	Inhabitants and invaders	17
3	The military occupation	25
4	Civil development: Claudius to Nero	33
5	The proto-palace and its context	39
6	The building of the Flavian palace	49
	The West Wing	53
	The North Wing	64
	The South Wing	80
	The East Wing	82
7	The gardens and the environment	91
8	The owner and his changing fortunes	105
9	The second century	111
10	The third century	135
11	Fire and destruction	141
12	Aftermath	147
Glossary		151
Visiting the site		153
Further reading		155
Index		157

List of illustrations

Black and white figures

1 Fishbourne from the air	12
2 The Fishbourne-Chichester region	18
3 The upper reaches of Chichester Harbour	26
4 The military granary	27
5 Reconstruction of the granary	27
6 The Claudian military buildings	29
7 Copper alloy fittings from military equipment	30
8 The Neronian civil buildings	34
9 Timber buildings 4 and 5 – the first timber house	35
10 Reconstruction of timber buildings 4 and 5	36
11 The site c.AD 70	41
12 The Neronian proto-palace	42
13 Ornate Corinthian capital	43
14 The location of the palace	50
15 Plan of the Flavian palace and its formal garden	51
16 The West Wing of the Flavian palace	53
17 Architectural reconstruction of the audience chamber	55
18 The audience chamber in the centre of the West Wing	56
19 The garden front of the audience chamber	57
20 The mosaic floor of corridor W13	58
21 Reconstruction of the mosaic in room W3	59
22 The mosaic in room W3	60
23 The mosaic in room W6	61
24 Reconstruction of the mosaic in room W8	62
25 The mosaic in room W8	63
26 Reconstruction of the mosaic in room W22	64
27 The North Wing of the Flavian palace	65
28 Reconstruction of the mosaic in room N1	66
29 Reconstruction of the mosaic in room N3	67
30 The mosaic in room N3	68

List of illustrations

31	The mosaic in room N4	69
32	General view across the west end of the North Wing of the palace	70
33	Reconstruction of the mosaic in room N7	71
34	Fragments of a stucco moulding found in the North Wing	72
35	The mosaic in room N13	73
36	Reconstruction of the mosaic in room N12	75
37	The mosaic in room N12	76
38–9	Motifs incorporated into the mosaic in room N12	77
40–41	The mosaic in room N20	79
42	Architectural reconstruction of the entrance hall in the East Wing	84–5
43	Architectural reconstruction of the aisled hall	86–7
44	The piers of the aisled hall	88
45	North colonnade in the north-east corner of the formal garden	92
46	The north-west corner of the formal garden of the Flavian palace	93
47	The north-west corner of the main formal garden of the palace	94
48	Column capital found in the East Wing of the palace	95
49	Bedding trench flanking the central path in the formal garden	96
50	The north-east corner of the formal garden	97
51	Reconstruction of the Flavian palace and its formal garden	99
52	The extent of the Flavian palace showing the Southern Garden	102
53	A marble head of a youth	106
54	The Togidubnus inscription from Chichester	108
55	The bath suite and exercise hall in the North Wing	122
56	The Medusa mosaic inserted into room N13	114
57	The Medusa mosaic in room N13 as originally found	115
58	The mid second-century baths in the East Wing	117
59	Courtyard in the East Wing	118
60	Courtyard in the East Wing	119
61	The second-century bath suite in the East Wing	120
62	Reconstruction of the mid second-century baths	121
63	The west end of the North Wing	122
64	General view of the west end of the North Wing	123
65	The second-century mosaic in room N14	124
66	The border of the Cupid mosaic in room N7	125
67–8	The two sea-horses from the Cupid mosaic	126
69	A cantharos from the Cupid mosaic	127
70	Part of the border of the Cupid mosaic	128
71	The development of the North Wing	131
72	The west courtyard in the North Wing	136
73	Roman well in the southern courtyard of the East Wing	137
74	The consolidation of wall plaster	144
75	Post-Roman burial	148

List of illustrations

Colour plates (between pp. 64–5)

1 General view of the military store building
2 The bridge by which the northern road crossed the stream
3 General view across the North Wing of the palace looking west
4 General view across the North Wing of the palace looking east
5 The Flavian mosaic in room N20
6 The Flavian mosaic in room W7
7 The Flavian mosaic in room N21
8 Part of a frieze of moulded stucco from the North wing of the palace
9 Fragment of painted wall plaster from the proto-palace
10 Fragment of a Roman wall painting dating to the early Flavian period
11 Coloured marbles fallen onto a tessellated floor
12 *Opus sectile* elements
13 Part of the West Wing from the apse of the audience chamber
14 View across the centre of the formal garden
15 General view of the replanted garden as it is now
16 The garden paths lined by bedding trenches
17 The extreme north-west corner of the garden
18 Colonnade and stylobate on the north side of the garden
19 The Cupid mosaic in room N7
20 Sea panther from the Cupid mosaic
21 Central roundel from the Cupid mosaic
22 Superimposed mosaics in room N13 about AD 100. The earlier floor can be seen in patches through holes in the later
23 Second-century mosaic in room N5
24 Second-century mosaic in the southern half of room N11
25 Third-century mosaic in the southern part of room N8
26 The channelled hypocaust system in room N1

The *cover illustration* shows the Cupid mosaic in the North Wing of the Palace.

Preface

The rediscovery of the Roman Palace at Fishbourne in 1960, and its excavation and display completed within the decade, took place in an age of innocence — a time well before the 'professionalization' of the discipline and the creation of the large commercial units which are so much a part of the excavation scene today. It was an age when local initiative dealt with local archaeological problems. The entire Fishbourne excavation of 1961–9 was organized by a group of volunteers — the Chichester Civic Society. It was carried out over a period of 50 weeks by an estimated 900 unpaid amateur diggers at a total cost of £11,000 — a sum raised entirely by the local society. At the beginning the future was uncertain because of the impending sale of the land for building development but at the crucial moment a Sussex archaeologist, Ivan Margary, came to the rescue by purchasing the entire site and vesting it in the Sussex Archaeological Society together with a substantial benefaction to pay for the construction of a cover building over the North Wing and a museum. As the project took shape, the building going hand in hand with the excavation, the *Sunday Times* joined in, financing and overseeing the planting of the garden and the layout of the museum exhibition. Work was completed on schedule and on 28 May 1968 the Roman Palace and its Garden were opened to the public. The publication of the two-volume report, together with the first edition of this book, in 1971 brought the first stage of the Fishbourne story to an end.

It had been a breathless period of ceaseless activity made memorable not only by a quite staggering succession of remarkable discoveries but by the exuberant spirit of cooperation that prevailed throughout. Fishbourne and the 1960s is a time that many of us look back on with nostalgia and wonder, thankful that we were young and energetic at the time.

Since its opening in 1968 Fishbourne has been managed with skill and care by the Sussex Archaeological Society and now regularly attracts 60,000 visitors a year.

In more recent times Fishbourne and its immediate hinterland has been the scene of renewed archaeological activity. The 1980s saw several significant excavations within the palace itself undertaken by the Curator, David Rudkin. The interventions were caused partly by the need to undertake remedial action to consolidate mosaics, but good use was made of an opportunity, caused by change of ownership, to explore the hitherto unknown southern part of the West Wing. At the same time the long-awaited construction of the trunk road in the field immediately to the east of the palace provided the occasion for Alec Down to demonstrate the enormous archaeological potential of the area in an arduous but rewarding rescue excavation. Since then, at various times throughout the 1990s, archaeological work, preceding building development to the east of the trunk road, has shown dense Roman occupation to extend some way towards Chichester.

A new era opened for Fishbourne in 1995 with the first season of a major excavation focused on a first-century masonry building lying between the palace and the trunk road. The work is a project of the Sussex Archaeological Society and is designed both to explore important research questions and to provide training for a new generation of volunteers.

To revise a book written nearly 30 years ago was a somewhat unnerving task. The initial intention had been simply to update it to take into account new discoveries and changed perceptions. This I have done, omitting the old Chapter XI on Everyday Life to keep the book within reasonable limits of size and price, but I have not been able to resist the temptation to make a number of minor changes of style, excising indulgences that I no longer find acceptable. As a result, I hope the text will read more easily.

I have been helped and generously encouraged by David Rudkin, Curator of The Fishbourne Roman Palace and by John Manley, Chief Executive of the Sussex Archaeological Society. Martin Henig has, as always, been a fund of sound advice and I have been greatly assisted in preparing a clean text and set of illustrations by my colleagues at the Institute, Alison Coveley, Lynda Smithson, Alison Wilkins and Bob Wilkins. To all I offer my grateful thanks. Their help has made what could have been a labour, a pleasure.

Barry Cunliffe
Institute of Archaeology
Oxford
7.i.98

1. Discovery

'There can be no doubt,' wrote the local historian Horsfield in 1835, 'that the Roman patricians and chiefs had villas in this neighbourhood, which time will some day bring to light.' He was right but the day was a long way off. In fact it was not until 1960 that the first hints of a Roman palatial building began to emerge from the fields of Fishbourne (**1**).

The first recorded discoveries to which Horsfield was referring were made early in the nineteenth century when 'In digging by the roadside [i.e. north and south of the main west road, the old A27] was found in 1805 a tessellated pavement about $13\frac{1}{2}$ ft wide; the length was not ascertained as it ran under a hedge. In the middle of this, occupying a space about 2 feet in diameter was part of the base of a column. Immediately underneath the floor, paved with small black and white stones, was a fine spring.' It seems that these discoveries were made during the construction of a house for on Friday, 18 April 1806, at the Bull's Head, Fishbourne, the house in question was sold by auction, the notice of sale stating that in addition to being 'delightfully situated ... commanding pleasing views of the Harbour and a beautiful featured inland country', it could boast a 'Curious Roman pavement 13ft square'. The house presumably still stands over the South Wing of the Roman palace but which it is cannot now be ascertained. A few years later in 1812 'certain subterranean remains were found ... Whether they were of a hypocaust or cold bath is unknown for the discovery was imperfectly made and inaccurately reported' — James Dallaway's terse summary in his *A History of the Western Division of the County of Sussex* is all we know of these tantalizing discoveries.

There the matter rested. A few scraps came to light later in the nineteenth century including finds of Roman pottery and tiles from the area of the watercress beds south of the village, but little attention was paid to them. Early this century, however, Fishbourne was blessed with a highly active antiquarian clergyman, the Reverend N. Shaw, who set about collecting and recording the Roman remains in his parish. From the site of his Rectory, now a housing estate, a quantity of Roman material was salvaged and was reported in a letter to *The Times* in 1929 and as late as 1936 Mr Shaw was giving advice and encouragement to a local boy who had discovered a mosaic pavement at the end of his garden, a mosaic which is known now to have belonged to the West Wing of the Roman palace.

By the late 1930s, then, parts of the South and West Wings of the palace had been

1. (Cambridge Committee for Aerial Photography.) Fishbourne from the air, looking north, at low tide. The position of the two east-west creek ends shows up as low-lying waterlogged land. The palace lay astride the present main road, in the centre of the picture

seen, rubbish from the silt filling the Roman harbour to the south had been discovered in the watercress beds and occupation could be shown to extend along the main road towards Chichester. But no-one at this stage believed that all these fragments belonged to a single structure.

A new impetus was given to local archaeological interests when early in 1960 a skin-diver recovered quantities of Roman building rubbish from the Mill pond south of the village, near the harbour. It was later in that year that work began on the construction of a water-main which was to run through the fields north of the village towards the Chichester bypass and thence to Selsey. The driver of the machine digging the trench found that he was cutting through masses of ancient building rubble. He mentioned this to the engineer in charge who, thinking them to be part of a tile clamp, reported the find to the local archaeological committee. Two observers went out immediately to record the discovery and, much to their surprise, found not only masses of Roman roofing tiles but also walls and mosaic pavements sectioned by the trench. A rapid survey of the remains and the collection of quantities of pottery from the spoil heap was all that could be done before the trench had to be refilled. But now, for the first time, the position of a large Roman building at Fishbourne was exactly established and, more important, the associated pottery suggested that it belonged to a very early period in the Roman occupation.

The next step was how to follow up the discovery. The Chichester Civic Society, to whom a full report was made, decided to organize an exploratory excavation of the area and the following Easter a small team of students working for three weeks cut a series of trial trenches sufficient to determine in broad outline the history of the site. First there had been a series of timber buildings, then, in the late first century, the site was cleared and a very large masonry building erected, which later had undergone a series of alterations. The real shock was finding a large well-constructed masonry building of such an early date; more staggering still was that the building was floored with mosaics earlier than any previously found in England and clearly the product of immigrant craftsmen. While plans for an extended summer season of excavation were underway, it was learnt that the area was about to be offered for sale as building-land, which might well have meant the total destruction of large parts of the buried structures. It was under this threat that the first major excavation of 1961 was carried out. Excavation strategy was simple: to uncover as much of the plan of the masonry building as possible, to obtain more dating evidence for it and to impress the public with the significance of the site. A series of rapid trial trenches accomplished the main aims in six weeks. The skeleton plan of more than 300ft of building, dating to the period AD 75–80, was exposed, and seven mosaics were uncovered. One of these, the Dolphin mosaic, found on the last afternoon of the excavation, symbolized the mood of the first year: it was discovered in a narrow trial trench, pushed westwards into an unknown area, just wide enough to show the head of a centrally placed Cupid with sea beasts on either side of him, one emerging from the unexcavated soil, the other disappearing into it. From a public relations point of view there could hardly have been a more dramatic ending to the season.

Throughout the next year negotiations for the purchase of the land on behalf of the Sussex Archaeological Trust advanced well and by the summer of 1962, when the second season's work began, the future of the site seemed assured. Work could therefore be concentrated on the large-scale area excavation of the archaeologically important, but less spectacular, timber buildings which lay beneath the East Wing of the masonry building. Gradually it became possible to untangle the early history of the site, before the great Roman building was erected in the late first century obscuring everything.

In the following years the excavations took in new areas. In 1963 the North Wing from the Dolphin mosaic westwards was uncovered, together with part of the newly discovered West Wing and during the next season most of the remainder of the North and West Wings was exposed. In 1965 work concentrated on the audience chamber in the West Wing and the great entrance hall opposite in the East Wing, but now for the first time it was realised that the central courtyard, more than 250ft across, had been laid out as a great formal garden in the Roman period, the excavation of which was to last for two more years.

Until 1966 work had been largely concerned with that part of the Roman site which lay to the north of the main road on land belonging to the Sussex Archaeological Trust, but some limited trenching in the gardens of the houses south of the road, the general area of the 1805 finds, gradually led to the recovery of the plan of the bath suite which lay at the south end of the East Wing. Until this time, however, there was little evidence as to how the south side of the garden was treated. The problem was finally resolved in 1967 when the owner of one of the houses in the crucial area invited us to excavate in his garden. Within a very short time it was possible to trace the main lines of a hitherto unsuspected South Wing 300ft long and 70ft wide, closing the great courtyard on its southern side. Although very little further excavation could be carried out here because the main road covered most of the wing, it seemed at last that the principal limits of the palace had been reached. But this was not so. At Easter 1969, in response to the development of a housing estate over the rather marshy area south of the South Wing, a close watch was kept on the foundation trenches which were cut for the buildings and a number of exploratory trenches were dug for archaeological reasons. The results were indisputable. Instead of the palace ending on its South Wing, the Roman built-up area continued further south, incorporating another large garden, to the sea some 350ft away. In the mud and silt filling of the artificially created lagoon beyond were found quantities of leather and wooden objects in an excellent state of preservation.

The excavation of Fishbourne, in its later stages, ran parallel with the construction of protective buildings, a museum and the other facilities which were erected by the Sussex Archaeological Trust, so that the site could be put on permanent display to the public. At an early stage it was decided not to attempt any close reconstruction of the Roman superstructure. Instead a cover building of timber, glass and aluminium, designed in a blatantly non-Roman style, was erected exactly upon the footings of the North Wing of the Roman palace, the area containing the best preserved floors. The aim of the building was two-fold: to create a protective environment over the delicate Roman structures and to offer some idea of the mass, if not the detail, of the original Roman building when viewed from the outside.

After the cover building had been completed and the protective covering of soil removed from the Roman floors for the last time, work began on the complex process involved in consolidating and conserving the ancient features. Temperature and humidity control had to be finely adjusted to prevent the growth of algae and fungi, walls needed impregnation and those mosaics which had become loosened by centuries of root growth and worm action were carefully lifted and relaid. No attempt was made to repair holes or breaks in the patterned mosaics, but the red tessellated floors were reconstructed where areas were missing. To show the difference between the original work and the patches, newly laid tesserae were set in a waterproof cement so that they always appear drier than the originals. Another problem arose when the supply of loose

Roman *tesserae* ran out but new ones were quickly made by a mosaicist from Roman tiles and bricks, tumbled together for a while in a cement mixer to remove their fresh appearance.

Gradually the obstacles were overcome and in 1968 the site with its cover building, museum and replanted garden was opened to the public.

But the story of Fishbourne does not end there. The 1980s saw a flurry of new activity. Three of the second-century mosaics in the North Wing (rooms N7, N8 and N13) had to be lifted and reset to consolidate them. This provided a valuable opportunity to study the earlier Flavian floors beneath. Other remedial work about the site, in room N3 and over the proto-palace, also provided new detail but more far-reaching was the excavation of part of the southern half of the West Wing in 1987–8, made possible when no. 80 Fishbourne Road changed hands.

Beyond the palace the field to the east was the scene of extensive excavations in 1983 and 1985–6 in advance of the construction of the new A27, while archaeological evaluations to the east of the new road between 1992 and 1995 have demonstrated Roman occupation to extend some distance towards Chichester. The excavations of 1983–6 showed that much of the area immediately to the east of the palace had been laid out for cultivation in the late first century but before this the site had been occupied by a masonry building. This structure, of great interest to the early history of the site, was chosen as the focus of a carefully planned research excavation which began in 1995.

The work of the last 30 years has shown how much more there is still to learn of Fishbourne in the Roman period. Only now are we beginning to appreciate the complexity of the landscape of which the palace was a part. There is still an immense amount to be discovered.

2. Inhabitants and invaders

The upper reaches of the Chichester Inlet had for a long time been attractive to man, for they provided safe anchorage, a plentiful supply of fish and wildfowl and gently shelving beaches suitable for the extraction of salt. The earliest trace of human activity at Fishbourne came in the form of two flint axes of the Mesolithic period, dating to the fifth or fourth millennium BC. One was found in the deep silt of the inlet. Presumably the harbour end was frequented by Mesolithic hunters in search of food, and traces of a temporary settlement have been found on dry land to the east of the palace.

The need of primitive societies for salt is clearly reflected in the archaeology of the harbours of the Solent where traces of evaporation pans, clay supports and flues connected with the Iron Age salt extraction are frequently found. At Fishbourne a few fragments of this briquetage have been recorded from an early beach level but so far no trace of extensive activity is known. On the dry land nearby, however, pottery of the first century BC has turned up in small quantities which suggests the use of the harbour area by Late Iron Age communities, but whether because of its sea communications, salt-producing facilities or simply its fertile hinterland, cannot be said.

For fifty years or so before Caesar's invasions of Britain in 55 and 54 BC the society of south and east Britain was changing rapidly, partly as the result of an influx of new peoples arriving from the turmoil on the adjacent continent and partly because of internal conflict. Innovations introduced during this period include a coin economy, the use of the wheel for turning pottery, and many other technological improvements. One development of some significance, which appeared at this time in parts of south-eastern Britain, was the use of massively-constructed linear earthworks, dividing off large tracts of land. Often these earthworks run from one river valley to another, but sometimes they would end apparently without reason. A splendid series of earthworks of this class divide up the coastal plain for miles around Chichester, running east–west across the gravel plain from one river valley to the next and north–south from the edge of the chalk downs to the sea **(2)**. It has been suggested that the earthworks were designed primarily against the chariot warfare which had been developed to a fine art by the late pre-Roman Iron Age. If so it would explain why they stopped on the thickly wooded valleys and on other forested zones through which vehicles could not pass.

The Chichester Entrenchments were evidently designed to protect not only the hinterland around the site of the later town of Chichester, but also the harbours of the

Inhabitants and invaders

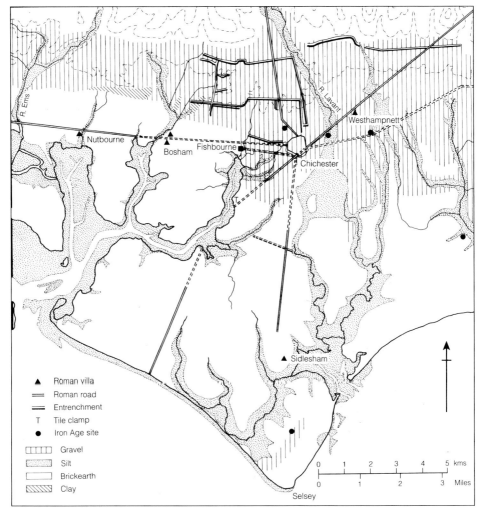

2 The Fishbourne-Chichester region

Fishbourne region and the whole of the Selsey peninsula to the south, which aerial photography has shown was covered with acres of early field systems. It is tempting to see the light brickearth soils of the peninsula as the principal arable land, while the clayey gravels further north were left to scrub and woodland to provide grazing and pannage for the flocks and herds. Within this territory would have been the main settlement nucleus possibly once somewhere in the area south of the present position of Selsey Bill. Massive coastal erosion has swept away many square miles of land even in historical times and in all probability the principal pre-Roman settlement has long since disappeared into the sea. All that has remained is a wide selection of gold coins washed up from time to time on the shore. Selsey was not the only settlement within the defended territory: a number of others, possibly individual farms, are known in the region. But there is no evidence to suggest that a major settlement of this date occupied the site of Chichester itself.

The political situation in Britain in the century before the invasion of AD 43 was, to say the least, complex. Ruling households rose to power from which individual kings would emerge to govern for a time before dying or being deposed. Sometimes they followed pro-Roman policies, at other times they were anti-Roman. This, and no doubt other causes, led to constant warring between tribes and also, apparently, quarrelling within the tribes, but how far these dynastic events affected the average peasant farmer is very difficult to assess. Life for the bulk of the population probably continued much as before no matter which political party was in power.

The general trend in policies and allegiances can be tolerably well pieced together using the evidence provided by changing types of coins, together with the occasional references to the British scene found in the contemporary classical sources. The earliest ruler of central southern Britain whose name survives is Commius, first a friend and later an avowed enemy of Caesar, who narrowly escaped assassination by fleeing to Britain from Gaul, apparently to join his people who had already settled here. The distribution of his coins suggests control over the area stretching from the middle Thames valley south into Hampshire and West Sussex, the territory belonging to the tribe known as the Atrebates.

Commius ruled until about 20 BC when he was succeeded by Tincomarus. At first Tincomarus issued coins of traditional form, each depicting a triple-tailed horse, but some time soon after 16 BC the design changed and a totally new type was introduced, copying a Roman *denarius* minted by the Emperor Augustus between 15 and 12 BC. These coins are so close to the original Roman model that a Roman engraver must have been employed to cut the die. This change may well have marked a complete turnabout in policy from the strong anti-Roman tradition of Commius to a new pro-Roman attitude. Some supporting evidence is provided by contemporary Roman writers: in 27 BC Dio tells us that the Britons would not come to terms with Rome, whereas Horace, in an ode published in 13 BC, refers to Caesar's suppliants in Britain. Presumably, therefore, the tough anti-Roman line of some at least of the British rulers had softened during this period: Tincomarus may well have been one.

But such a *volte-face* could not have been easy for the older members of the Atrebatic aristocracy to accept. There seems to have been trouble, for by AD 7 Tincomarus had found it necessary to flee to the protection of the emperor in Rome. He was succeeded by Epillus who styled himself *Rex* on his coins, implying perhaps some form of imperial recognition from Rome. But his rule over the Atrebates was short and although he appears to have continued to issue coins in Kent, the old kingdom seems soon to have passed to Verica.

If the coin evidence is reliable, Verica maintained close connections with Roman culture, continuing to use the title *Rex* and copying coins of Tiberius. He even at one stage introduced the vine-leaf emblem to demonstrate, some suggest, his preference for Roman wine. All the time imported Roman goods continued to reach the kingdom through ports such as Poole Harbour and probably Selsey.

In other parts of Britain policies were different. In the Thames valley and eastern Britain were the hostile warlike Catuvellauni, who were later to lead military opposition against the Roman armies. From about AD 25 there is some evidence to suggest that their influence was beginning to expand southwards into Atrebatic territory eroding Verica's sphere of influence.

The end of Verica's rule came in about AD 42, when at last the old king was forced to flee the country and run to the Emperor Claudius for support. Superficially it might appear that external military factors finally dislodged him, but it may be that dissident elements within the Atrebates were responsible — we are unlikely ever to know. At any event, the general political situation in 42–3 is clear enough: the Chichester region with its superb harbours was still largely pro-Roman in attitude and moreover, since it was now under pressure from its enemies, it had come to rely heavily upon Roman support. To the north, in eastern Britain, the Thames valley and spreading into Wiltshire, were the hostile Catuvellauni, now closely aligned with the Dobunni further west in Gloucestershire; west of the River Test and extending across Dorset into Devon and Somerset, was another anti-Roman tribe, the Durotriges. Thus, in a broad arc from Kent to Dorset, lived those opposed to Rome and her policies. The situation in east Kent and east Sussex is less clear, but again the general appearance is of opposition. With his diminishing kingdom hedged in by enemies on three sides and the sea on the fourth, it is hardly surprising that the ageing Verica looked to Rome, the traditional ally of his people, for help.

On the Roman side, Verica's flight was opportune. Britain had always been shrouded with an air of mystery; there were rumours of great mineral wealth but more important it served as a haven for dissidents who could conveniently sail across to Gaul to cause trouble for the Roman government. For these reasons, and no doubt for personal glorification, Caesar had led two military expeditions into the country in 55 and again in 54 BC. Even his own accounts of the events hardly cover up the near disasters which he experienced, but, while in a military sense the expeditions failed, politically he could claim to have supported friendly tribes against aggressors and extracted a promise of annual tribute. He may well have intended to return again to carry out a more thorough job but pressing problems arose to require his presence elsewhere. The Britons were left to themselves and soon the tribute to Rome ceased to be paid. Augustus was uneasy about the British situation: it was an irritant but of minor importance compared with some of his problems, and so long as diplomatic relations could be kept going he was content to leave things much as they were. By the time Gaius had come to power, Britain had taken on a new significance in the minds of Roman politicians. Massive military preparations were put in hand at Boulogne, a fleet was built and the harbour remodelled. But all this came to nothing when the recalcitrant army was led to the seashore by Gaius and made to pick up sea-shells as a mark of his contempt for their mutinous fear of Britain. Nevertheless the fleet and the naval installations remained.

When, in AD 41, Claudius rather unexpectedly became emperor, he began to consider Britain with growing interest. To consolidate his rather shaky position he needed a military triumph in Rome, but to become eligible for so high an honour it was necessary to annex a new territory for the Empire with a minimum loss of Roman life. Britain was the obvious area. It was relatively near at hand and suitable preparations had, after all, been made by Gaius. Pride came into this too: Britain was always something of an embarrassment to Rome after Caesar had established an interest in the island. The Britons would not come to terms; such arrogance could hardly be allowed to remain so close to the Empire.

The arrival of Verica in Rome may have been the deciding factor: the ruler of one of Rome's oldest British allies was seeking help. A British campaign could now be presented in terms of Rome's support for her friends in their time of need. More important, Verica must have brought with him an intimate knowledge not only of the country but of the detailed political situation. Such intelligence would have been essential for the planning of a successful operation.

In AD 43, after an inauspicious beginning during which the troops, fearful of the sea and what lay beyond, at first refused to budge, the invasion force set sail from Boulogne under the command of Aulus Plautius. It was split into three arms, says the historian Cassius Dio, so that a unified landing would not be opposed. This statement, and the fact that Dio says that after some trouble ships were guided west by a comet, has led some historians to suggest that the invasion force was divided into three prongs aimed at widely spaced beach-heads around the south-east shores of Britain. While the usually accepted view is that the landings all took place in Kent, where Richborough became the main supply base, a compelling case can be made for suggesting that the main landing took place in the harbours of the Solent with the Fishbourne/Chichester region as the focus. This would fit well with the geography implied by Dio and would make good strategic and political sense. Where better for the invasion to begin than in the heart of Verica's territory where the Roman army might expect a friendly reception? From here one force could march through the Weald to cross the Thames and take the main centre of Catuvellaunian resistance at Camulodunum (Colchester) while the second legion, led by Vespasian, could concentrate on subduing the Isle of Wight and the West Country. The recent discovery that Stane Street, the Roman road thought to run from Chichester to London, in fact began well south of the later Roman town to the south of Dell Quay on the harbour-edge, adds some support to the theory of a military landing in the area, suggesting that the road was laid out as the military communication joining the harbour to the Thames crossing at London, in the consolidation phase following the initial landing and advance. It may have been in this second phase that the supply base was established at Richborough, linked to London by Watling Street. The suggestion that the invasion force chose to land at the principal Atrebatic harbour has much to commend it but the matter must remain in the realms of debate pending more archaeological work.

The political stabilization of the Atrebatic kingdom was important to the early consolidation of the province, particularly as an example to neighbouring tribes of how the Romans treated their friends and allies. First the occupying authorities would have needed a figure-head at the same time acceptable to the natives and manageable by Rome. Verica, the obvious choice, does not seem to have returned. By 43 he would have been a very old man, if indeed he was still alive. If it was internal dissent that forced him to run to Rome, to return such a man would have been ill-advised. In the event the person singled out to replace him was Tiberius Claudius Togidubnus, a shadowy but intensely interesting personality who dominated the Chichester region for more than thirty years after the invasion, and with whose fortunes the early history of Fishbourne was probably closely bound. Traditionally he has been known as Cogidubnus, following the mention of his name in the text of Tacitus' *Agricola*, but recent scholarship has suggested that the more appropriate reading should be Togidubnus. It is this preferred spelling that we adopt in this book.

Our slight factual knowledge of Togidubnus comes from two sources. The Roman historian Tacitus, writing of him, says that 'he maintained his unswerving loyalty to our own times' and that certain cantons (estates) were given to him. The second source is a remarkable inscription carved on Purbeck marble, which was dug up near the centre of Chichester in 1723 **(54)**. It records the erection of a Temple of Neptune and Minerva to the honour of the Divine Household, that is the household of the emperor, by a guild of craftsmen. It was erected with the authority of Tiberius Claudius Togidubnus, who is given the title of *rex magnus Brit* — 'great king of the Britons'. Together these two sources strongly suggest that Togidubnus was a client king responsible for the area in which Chichester is situated. His name, incorporating the Celtic *dubno* or *dumno* meaning powerful or deep, clearly implies that he was a native but had been granted Roman citizenship under Claudius, whose first names he adopted. The people living in the Chichester region soon became known as the *Regnenses* ('the people of the kingdom') and the new Roman town which grew up at Chichester was called *Noviomagus Regnensium* ('the new market [or clearing] of the people of the kingdom'), implying that the town replaced an old centre which may have been at Selsey. The kingdom, then, over which Togidubnus ruled was the old Atrebatic territory to which additional areas were added.

That Togidubnus succeeded Verica is clear, but when and why? Unfortunately there can be no firm answers. One possibility is that he was a member of the ruling household, next in succession to Verica, who took over when the old man fled or perhaps he even ousted him. Alternatively, he may simply have been a promising young man picked out by the Romans as a potential leader when they landed, and set up to run the kingdom for them. There are, however, two things that can be said of him: he was successful and he seems enthusiastically to have embraced Roman culture from an early date. It is likely therefore that he was a member of the ruling household able to command respect and support, and that he was well versed in the Roman way of life.

Now, it was a general policy of the early emperors to encourage young men of noble families from the barbarian fringes to live in Rome, either as refugees from their homeland or as hostages, so that they could be inculcated with Roman culture and values. The return of such a policy for the Romans is self-evident: it appealed tremendously to Claudius, always the shrewd manipulator. One instance of its practical value is well documented: the Cherusci, a German tribe who lived north of the Rhine frontier, emerged from a period of bitter civil war, having slaughtered their aristocracy. The only surviving member of the nobility was a young prince, Italicus, nephew of the famous German war-lord Arminius. His mother had been held hostage and he had been born and reared in Rome, as a Roman. When the Cherusci appealed to Claudius to send them a leader, Claudius selected Italicus, reminding him that he was the first man born in Rome as a Roman citizen to rule a foreign throne. It is tempting to see in the life and aspirations of Togidubnus a similar Roman training. Perhaps he, too, had been taken to Rome as a child and educated there, to be returned to his homeland and people on the eve of the Roman conquest. We will never know, but this is part of the attraction which the man holds for us.

Speculation aside, it can be said that Togidubnus was installed as a client king at the beginning of the invasion period. Apart from maintaining the pro-Roman policies of his kingdom, his main function in the first weeks would have been to create a stable bridgehead for the advancing army and its supply lines. At the same time, by demonstrating the benefits of his allegiance with Rome, he would probably have attempted to win over neighbouring rulers, persuading them to offer their submission to the advancing legions. The Dobunni, whose capitulation is recorded in Dio's narrative, may well have submitted direct to Togidubnus; there were probably others, too, who were ready to throw in their lot with the invaders.

Was he, as some writers have said, a quisling or was he a man of vision, tired of petty tribal squabbles, who saw in Rome the possibility of a lasting peace and of a cultural life hitherto unknown in barbarous Britain?

3. The military occupation

The earliest buildings to be defined at Fishbourne belong to the period immediately following the invasion of AD 43; in form they suggest close connections with the military authorities. The attraction of the site clearly lay in the close proximity of a good harbour set in a well-protected position at the head of a wide inlet (**1**). Originally the navigable waters would have been T-shaped in plan with a main north-south channel leading to two lateral channels set at right-angles to it (**3**). Of these only the eastern channel has been partly examined by excavation: the western channel has been modified by the construction of a large mill-pond which now fills much of its valley. Although excavation of this eastern inlet has been limited, we know that the shallow gravel-floored valley was cut by several channels kept free from silt by two freshwater streams flowing in from the north and east. Further to the south, in the main channel, there would have been deep-water anchorage for larger ships, well protected from storms and violent seas by twists and turns in the lower reaches of the creek. Such were the physical advantages of Fishbourne Harbour.

The main site to be excavated lay at the head of the eastern inlet. Here the clayey gravel subsoil sloped down gently to a gravel-floored valley, through which flowed a small stream barely 10ft across. The site as we now know it was divided into three zones by two parallel roads built of rammed gravel, both of which crossed the stream by means of fords. Excavations beneath the roads showed that they had been laid directly on the untouched soil before any signs of occupation rubbish had been allowed to accumulate. Two buildings of this early period were found and completely excavated, one lying between the roads, the other to the north of the northern road. Part of a third building was seen in a trial trench dug south of the southern road and part of another was noted to the east of the present stream.

The first building, an elongated structure more than 100ft long and 24ft wide, lay on a north–south axis between the two roads. As the ground plan shows (4), it was a complex structure based on a series of vertical timbers 6–9in in diameter, which had been set in six parallel trenches dug 2ft deep into the natural gravel. The verticals were kept in position by the spoil which had been tightly packed back into the trenches. Later, after the timbers had rotted, darker soil from above fell into the voids. Therefore when the excavation had reached the appropriate level it was possible to recognize three types of soil texture and colour: the tightly-packed undisturbed natural gravel, the looser

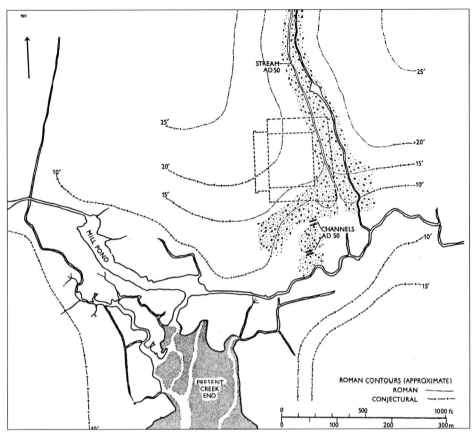

3 The upper reaches of Chichester Harbour. The position of the Flavian palace is shown by the broken line

gravelly soil packed back into the trenches and a much darker soil filling the old post-holes. On this basis, although the building had completely disappeared, its plan was recoverable by excavation.

Since the vertical timbers were spaced closely together, on a grid about 3ft apart, they could not have stood to the full height of the building. It is almost certain, therefore, that they were no more than piles projecting 2–3ft above the soil to take a platform of joists, upon which the rest of the building was erected. Raised floors of this kind are a well-known feature of the Roman military buildings used as granaries (**5**), the floor serving two functions: to keep the corn above the damp ground and well ventilated, and to prevent the easy approach of rodents. Exactly how the superstructure was designed cannot now be discovered, but all that was required was some simple form of single storied erection with walls strong enough to take the thrust of grain piled up against them. Judging by the amount of tile fragments lying around, the roof was tiled, no doubt to reduce the risk of fire. The north end of the building was more simply constructed than the rest, without the close-spaced rows of piles. The explanation for this would seem to be that the area formed part of a covered loading bay.

The structure of the building implies that it served the specialized function of a granary. Granaries of this general type are well known on Roman military sites, usually

The military occupation

4 Timber building 1 – the military granary

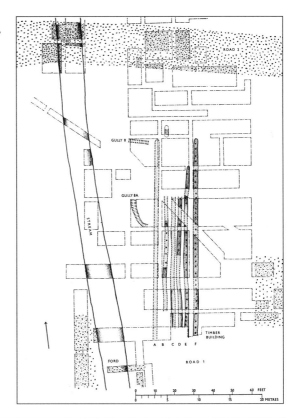

5 Suggested reconstruction of the granary (by Nigel Sunter)

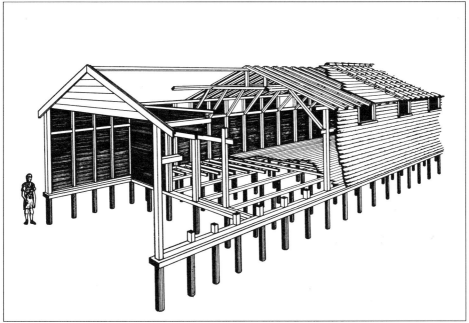

built in masonry, but in Britain more than twelve similar timber structures were found at the early military supply base at Richborough.

The second timber building fronted onto the northern road (**6**). Again it was constructed of timbers but this time they were set individually in post pits about 3ft in diameter and of equivalent depth, spaced at about 8–9ft intervals (**Col 1**), forming a building about 100ft by 50ft. The posts probably supported a raised timber floor since no trace of a floor level or of any form of wear could be found on the surface of the original soil beneath. It may be that the vertical timbers continued to the full height of the building so that they could be used as a basis for internal partitions. An arrangement of this kind would have been useful if the interior had been divided into bins for loose grain. The rows of timbers on the north and south sides of the building were less regularly spaced than the others, possibly because they formed some kind of veranda or covered loading platform. The gravel of the northern road was laid right up to the south side, probably to create a metalled apron so that carts could easily turn round, pass each other or back up to the unloading area. The north side of the building was also flanked by a gravelled area 15ft wide, which had been provided with shallow side ditches to facilitate drainage. This tends to support the idea of a veranda along the north side, but it can never have been used for major loading and unloading like the south front. Parallels to the building are by no means common, but the little fort built into the corner of the Iron Age hillfort at Hod Hill in Dorset has a granary constructed in an almost identical fashion though the posts are a little more closely spaced.

What has been described can only be a small part of a very much larger settlement, the full extent of which is so far unknown.

The date at which the buildings were erected cannot be given with absolute precision, for the archaeological material does not allow close dating. Nevertheless the base was laid out on a site which had not been previously occupied, and from the earliest occupation layers associated with them come quantities of coins and pottery of the types in use at the very beginning of the Roman occupation of Britain. Some of the pottery, in particular certain of the samian ware (pottery with a distinctive glossy red fabric manufactured in Gaul) is found on continental sites dating to the late 30s and early 40s of the first century AD. It would not normally be expected to occur in this country much after 45.

The coins also point to early military beginnings. Two main types are found: the small silver *denarii* used to pay the soldiers, often old worn coins still in use after 40 or 50 years of service, and the larger bronze issues (*asses*) of Claudius, of which more than 60 have been recovered from the early levels at Fishbourne. Most of these are copies struck in this country, probably under contract to the army, to overcome a shortage of small change. The Claudian copies occur in large numbers on early military sites but continue to be used well into the Neronian period.

Besides the pottery, coins and other trinkets commonly found on Roman sites, both civil and military, several objects of military equipment have been recovered (**7**). These include a decorated belt-plate, belt buckles and several small strap buckles and strap hinges from military uniforms. The only weapon of distinctly military type to be found is the head of an iron ballista bolt exactly like those known to have been fired by the Roman army in great volleys at the native defenders of the hillforts of Hod Hill and Maiden Castle. But perhaps the most interesting piece of military equipment from

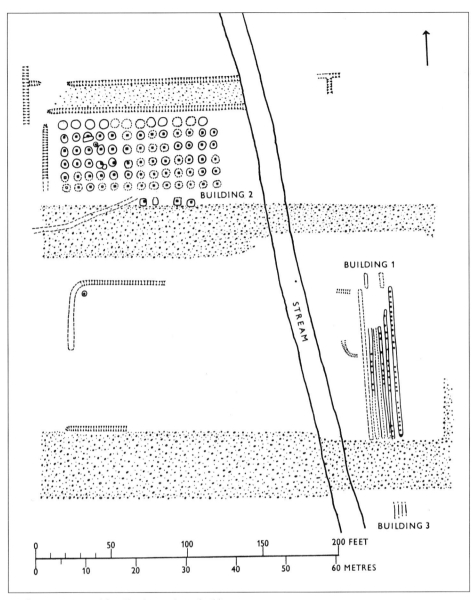

6 The arrangement of the Claudian military buildings

Fishbourne is a bronze legionary's helmet which was dredged up from the harbour in the nineteenth century, and is now in the British Museum. The helmet is well preserved and still retains its wide neck-flap to protect the neck from sword slashes and the visor above the forehead to deflect glancing blows from the face. It is tempting to think of it as being dropped overboard by a legionary about to disembark.

There is, then, reasonable evidence for a military supply base at the head of Fishbourne Harbour at the beginning of the Roman invasion in AD 43, but before considering the wider implications of this it is necessary to say something of the nature

The military occupation

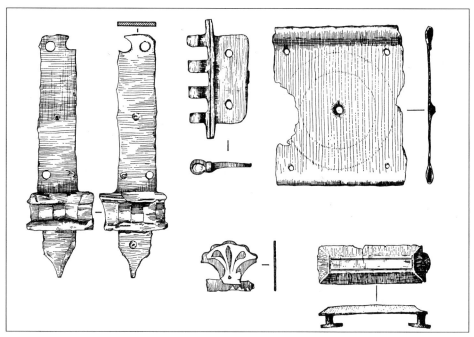

7 Copper alloy fittings from military equipment

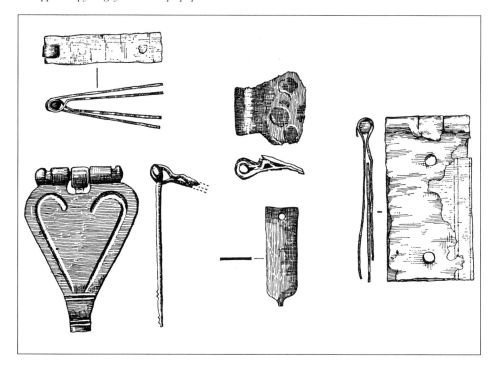

of the base and its relationship to Chichester. The excavation has demonstrated the existence of several store buildings together with facilities for barges to unload or load nearby. The remains, as we know them at present, are clearly part of a specialized installation in all probability the warehouses of a military harbour. Where the main fort lies is not yet clear but the most likely location is somewhere beneath Chichester. While it is true that no incontrovertible evidence of military building has yet come to light beneath the city, excavations are gradually amassing an impressive array of very early occupation levels and a substantial early ditch, which could be military, has been found beneath the later cremation-cemetery which grew up outside the East gate of the later Roman town. Add to this a number of pieces of bronze military equipment, recovered mainly from the eastern part of the walled area, and the evidence for military occupation begins to look impressive.

The presence of military remains at Fishbourne and Chichester dating to the time of the invasion raises a number of interesting strategic and political questions. While it could be argued that a small peace-keeping force would have been advantageous to Togidubnus at the beginning of the occupation, the excavated remains suggest something far more substantial. As we have seen an attractive, though theoretical, case can be made out for the suggestion that Chichester Harbour was the site of one of the military landings in AD 43. But even if this suggestion is not accepted it is tolerably certain that Fishbourne played a significant part in the conquest of the hostile south-west spearheaded by the second legion led by Vespasian. The Isle of Wight was taken, two powerful tribes were overcome and more than twenty fortified native capitals destroyed. The friendly enclave of Togidubnus' kingdom would have been a very sensible place to create a base, the more so because of its excellent harbours protected from the winds and storms coming from the south by the land mass of the Isle of Wight. Good harbours would have been essential because any conquest of south-western Britain would have entailed the use of extensive naval support to bring up troops and supplies to the line of battle.

Whatever their origins the military installations in the Fishbourne/Chichester region would have provided the principal supply base from which more westerly bases could be served by sea, bases such as those at Hamworthy in Poole Harbour, at Topsham near Exeter, and the suspected bases near Weymouth and at Bitterne. The Fishbourne store buildings close to the harbour would have been suitable for the protection of corn and other commodities in transit, whilst the remains beneath Chichester might have belonged to a camp for reserve troops or even the winter quarters to which the field army could withdraw at the end of the first season's operations.

Vespasian's campaign against the Durotriges and probably the Dumnonii, the tribes occupying west Hampshire, Dorset, south Somerset and Devon, and the destruction of their principal fortified settlements was probably rapid and may well have been accomplished within the first two campaigning seasons, but the situation was an uneasy one and forts such as those at Hod Hill, Waddon Hill and elsewhere had to be built for the permanent garrisons left to keep an eye on the native tribesmen.

By 47, south-east Britain was regarded as conquered and a densely fortified frontier zone had been constructed on either side of the Fosseway — a military communication road running from Lincoln to the Devon coast east of Exeter. Even though the forts remained in Durotrigian territory, it is unlikely that the military installations of

The military occupation

Fishbourne and Chichester were required any longer — the new network of inland communications would have rendered them obsolete and the land they occupied could have been returned to its original owners.

4. Civil development: Claudius to Nero

When the army finally moved away from the area, they left behind them a well-fitted harbour at Fishbourne and an excellent system of roads converging on the Chichester region, for it is probable that Stane Street, the road linking Chichester Harbour to London, and the coast road west from Chichester were laid out initially by the military authorities. The presence of the army would also have encouraged camp followers to set up their stalls nearby, providing for the needs of the soldiers at a price. The military establishment, then, created a situation favourable to urban growth and as soon as the soldiers moved off civilian development began to flourish. Similar processes lay behind the growth of many of the Roman towns in England and on the continent.

How long it took the new developments around the route node at Chichester to usurp the position of the old market at Selsey it is difficult yet to say, but we must imagine a steady drift towards the new centre. Archaeology has little yet to show of the early stages in the growth of the town, but some of the streets would have been laid out, flanked by timber buildings, traces of which have turned up on the east side of North Street. A substantial masonry building found in 1740 at the corner of St Martins Lane and East Street may also be of this early date, for lying in the rubble was found an inscription of well-cut letters carved on a slab of Purbeck marble 3ft by $2\frac{1}{2}$ ft. Although it has since been lost, the lettering is recorded to have read 'For Nero Claudius Caesar Augustus, son of the deified Claudius, grandson of Germanicus Caesar, great grandson of Tiberius Caesar Augustus, great great grandson of the deified Augustus, in his fourth year of Tribunician power, four times acclaimed Imperator, consul for the fourth time by decree of the Senate, the vow was deservedly fulfilled.' The stone, a dedicatory inscription, is an impressive tribute to the Emperor Nero. It may well be a result of Togidubnus' go-ahead policy of forcing Romanization on his people. The inscription alone shows that by the year 58 the community was fast developing a decidedly Roman aspect.

At Fishbourne the changes can be more closely followed. One of the first alterations to be made to the military layout was to the road system. The southern road was abandoned and the ford by which it crossed the stream was dug away to allow the stream to flow faster in order to improve the drainage of the valley above. The northern road, however, was retained but because of the dampness of the land hereabouts side ditches were dug along part of its length to remove surface water and drain it into the stream.

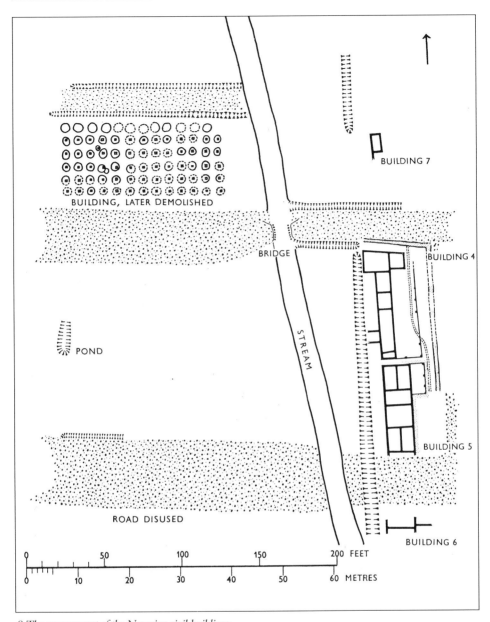

8 The arrangement of the Neronian civil buildings

At the stream-crossing a timber bridge was constructed (**Col 2**). It was quite narrow, barely 10ft wide, but a ford was provided by the side of it, perhaps to allow livestock and wheeled traffic to pass while pedestrians could cross more comfortably.

The principal building activity was concentrated in the area east of the stream (**8**), partly over the site of one of the old military store buildings. Here two completely new timber buildings were erected, both built on a framework of sill beams about a foot square, placed on the ground surface. Into these would have been slotted vertical

Civil development: Claudius to Nero

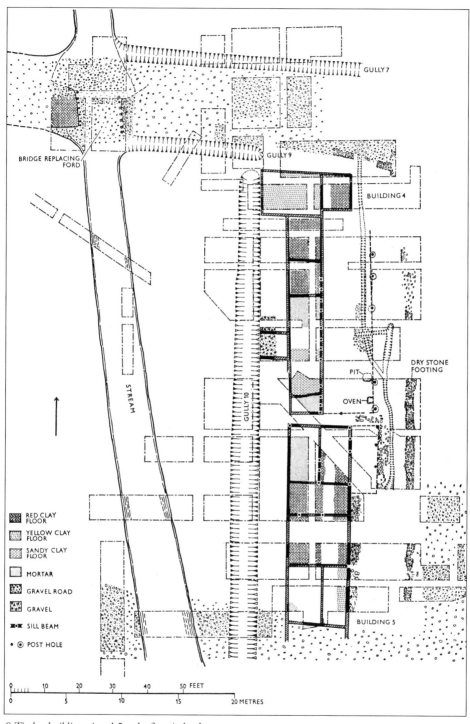

9 Timber buildings 4 and 5 – the first timber house

10 Suggested reconstruction of timber buildings 4 and 5 (by Nigel Sunter)

timbers to create the framework of the superstructure, the spaces between them being infilled with wattle and daub. Of the two buildings which have been almost totally excavated (**9**), the southern (building 4) was by far the more impressive with its seven rooms laid out in a single block 18ft wide by more than 60ft long flanked along part of the east side by a veranda. Each room had been carefully floored with mortar or clay and some, at least, of the walls had been thinly plastered and painted red and white.

The building which lay to the north was different both in style and function. It was composed simply of a range of five rooms constructed end on in a strip 10ft wide with two much larger rooms built across the north end to give a T-shaped ground plan. East of the range was a large working area which ran the length of the building and may have been roofed in one with it. The entrance to the working area lay towards its centre where stones and tiles were thrown down to prevent the constant tread of feet wearing the soil into hollows, which would soon have become puddles in wet weather. There is some evidence to suggest that a passageway led through the building opposite the entrance and gave access to what appears to be a bridge, constructed of massive horizontal timbers, over a wide drainage gully which ran the length of the building.

The rooms of the main range were floored with mortar and clay, but there was no trace of wall painting. The working area in front was unfloored except for the rubble spread, but within the enclosure was a small oven with a fuel pit close by and near the oven was found a large lump of crude bronze, hinting at the possibility of metalworking.

Although the two buildings were separated from each other by a narrow passageway, they are clearly part of a unified plan, for both were fronted by a drystone footing more than 3ft wide, outside of which lay a north–south street. Exactly how the footing functioned it is difficult to say, but it may well have supported a continuous colonnade of timber or brick serving to unify the two structures. Similar colonnades, common to several buildings, are a well-known feature of Roman street architecture in this country.

A close parallel is provided by a row of early timber shops in the Roman town of Verulamium: their frontage onto Watling Street was lined by a spacious veranda which allowed pedestrians to walk for some distance under cover. A second unifying feature at Fishbourne was a wide drainage gully which ran the full length of the two buildings and must eventually have emptied into the stream.

The two buildings, then, are part of the same overall plan but are evidently of different functions (**10**). The southern building with its spacious rooms, painted walls and veranda would have been eminently suitable as a high-class dwelling, while the northern building was some kind of workshop with attached living quarters. It is tempting to see them as the main house and servants' range belonging to a single establishment of some status. By later standards the accommodation was somewhat meagre, but compared with contemporary Romano-British buildings the Fishbourne complex was positively luxurious. In addition to the two buildings just described, part of another of some size was found to the south of the road (unless, of course, it is part of building 4).

On the north side of the northern road stood the military store building, which by this time was no longer of much use. The main problem was that timber embedded in the ground tended to rot through just above ground level, where the dampness and the supply of air were optimum for the activities of the bacteria which destroy wood cells. Some of the uprights had completely rotted through and were removed, leaving stumps in position. Others, however, were still sufficiently sound to warrant digging out. It was probably late in the 50s that the store building was demolished and its site and that of the road to the north became blanketed with a thick layer of occupation refuse thrown out from the buildings to the south and east.

Immediately to the east of the old store house was a low-lying area alongside the stream. Several attempts were made to consolidate it with tips of stone and gravel but it remained open, perhaps as a yard. Further to the east, on drier land, a small timber building or shed was built, attached to a boundary fence, neither of which have been fully traced.

The area further to the north along the valley was evidently occupied by timber buildings, but excavations here have been confined to very limited trial trenching. How extensively this area was built up remains to be demonstrated, but at one point a timber-lined well was discovered. The mere existence of such a feature implies nearby habitation, but details must await large-scale excavation.

One final feature requires comment. In the north-west corner of the site a substantial ditch was found, measuring some 12ft wide and up to 6ft deep. It turned a right-angle beneath what was later to become the west end of the North Wing of the palace. Why so large a ditch was dug is not clear, nor can its extent be traced any further. At first a military origin seemed possible, but the pottery found in the primary silt of the ditch showed that it was open in the Neronian period, by which time the military occupation of the site had ceased. It may, perhaps, have served as a property boundary or for drainage, or a combination of the two.

The harbour to the south still played an important part in the life of the site. At this stage ships were coming in and jettisoning their ballast of stone boulders before taking on heavy cargoes. These boulders, found in some numbers in the early levels, derived mainly from the western sea-ways, coming from Cornwall, the Channel Islands and probably the Armorican peninsula.

It can be said, therefore, that in the decade or two following the invasion Fishbourne and Chichester developed rapidly from their early military beginnings, Chichester taking on the form of a small urban centre, while Fishbourne continued to serve as its port. At Fishbourne, however, a large private house was built which by the local standards of the time must have belonged to a person of some wealth. Whether it stood alone amid the harbour installations or is one of a group of private dwellings is a question which can only be answered by further extensive excavations.

5. The proto-palace and its context

Early in the 60s, during the reign of Nero, a significant change took place at Fishbourne: the timber house and its outbuildings were pulled down and replaced by a substantial masonry building planned in Roman style — called here the proto-palace for reasons which will later become evident. It is possible to trace in some detail how the preparations were made for the building and how gradually it took shape.

At an early stage, but possibly not right at the beginning, the timber buildings were demolished, any useful materials such as roof-tiles or timbers being stockpiled for later use. The ground sills upon which the old structure was based were apparently too rotten to warrant removal: one of them could still be traced in position, surviving now as a streak of brown spongy soil. The clay daub from the walls was generally spread about to level up the old site. It was at this stage that the stream was diverted into a new channel dug along the eastern limit of the building site, along the line now followed by the present-day stream. Its original bed was completely filled with clay and rubble derived from the building works. The next stage was the reconstruction of the southern road by remetalling the part passing across the gully and stream, and considerably widening it west of the stream. This road and the north–south road, which was also partly remetalled at this time, were used as the main service roads connected with the building work. Along them the building materials would have been brought in and, judging by the thickness of greensand chippings lying above the metalling, it was here that the ashlar blocks were probably tooled and stockpiled.

The area of the old timber buildings and the expanse of open land to the west was now enclosed by a fence constructed of large vertical timbers placed in individual post-pits. One row, running north–south, has been traced close to the eastern limit of the site. The second row, which joined it at approximately right-angles, ran along the southern side of the northern road, actually impinging upon the metalling. That the fence belongs to this period can be shown by the way in which its post-holes are cut through the destroyed walls and sill beams of the old building, while the posts were packed in position with large fresh blocks of stone of the type brought in to provide the decorative finishes to the new masonry proto-palace.

It was within the eastern part of the enclosure that much of the preparation work for the new building was carried out (**11**). The masons responsible for creating the decorative stone inlay used the area as their working yard, leaving behind them a thick litter of stone chippings, sand and partly finished objects, providing a unique insight into the processes used by the stone workers. Several types of stone were brought in as crude blocks, the commonest being a blue-grey Purbeck marble from Dorset, a hard white chalk which may also have come from the Purbeck hills in Dorset, a grey silt-stone probably from the Weald and a red silt-stone which has been identified as coming from somewhere around the Mediterranean. This particular stone is a laminated sedimentary rock, streaks of which are sometimes yellow or purple, colours which also proved to be attractive to the stone workers. Granular white Carrara marble from Italy was also imported at this time though in much smaller quantities, but a brown speckled marble from the Côte d'Or in eastern France occurred in relatively large amounts.

First of all the crude blocks of stone were tooled into regular shapes using a hammer to begin with and later various grades of chisels, ending up with an all-over pecking with a fine chisel point. Then followed the sawing of the blocks into sheets of various thicknesses ranging between an eighth of an inch to three-quarters of an inch. Pliny describes how this was carried out with a large multiple-bladed saw which cut a single block into a number of sheets in one operation. The iron saw blades were not generally toothed since a toothed blade would wear out too quickly. Instead strips of iron were used with a fine sand as an abrasive and water to lubricate the process. The sand grains, rubbed backwards and forwards by the blades, would soon have cut deeply into the stone. Pliny also mentions how some dishonest masons used a coarse sand to make wider cuts and thus used up the client's marble more quickly. That these processes were employed at Fishbourne is shown by the thick layers of fine white sand found all over the floor of the working area and by several broken blocks of stone which show the marks of the multiple-bladed saw.

After the sheet of stone had been produced, its upper surface was carefully smoothed, using rubbers of a hard ironstone, several of which still survive. Then the sheet was marked out with a scriber into the required shape. If, as was often the case with the Purbeck marble, the sheet was to be cut into strips or squares, the scribed line was usually pecked with a chisel to form a keying for a single-bladed saw. When the cut was nearly through, a quick hammer blow would detach the strip, leaving a burr along one edge (rather like breaking a bar of chocolate), which could easily be trimmed off with a hammer.

The general process, most commonly employed, has been outlined but it must be remembered that a wide variety of products were turned out by the yard. In addition to strips and geometric shapes of stone for floor inlay, marble mouldings were carved from Purbeck and Carrara marble for use in framing windows and doors. One area of the yard seems to have specialized in cutting small intricate shapes for a very fine inlay, probably for furniture, while in another area Purbeck marble mortars and pestles were being produced for use in the kitchen. In fact the masons were making the entire range of stone fittings for the new house, which was by this stage taking shape close by.

It is most likely that the yard was used by other craftsmen as well, such as the carpenters, whose contribution to the new building would have been no less than that of the masons. Large lumps of iron slag suggest the presence of iron smiths making the nails and other fittings for the complicated roof structure. Other products, like roof-tiles and bricks, would have been made in clamps close to the clay pits, such as those at Dell Quay, just south of Fishbourne, and brought to the site as finished products.

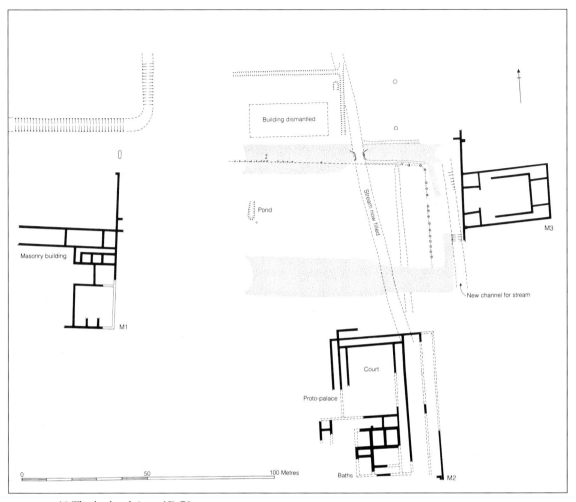

11 The developed site c. AD 70

While all these preparations were going on, the house itself was gradually rising, built in a fine ashlar masonry of greensand blocks set in hard cream-coloured mortar on footings of coursed stone blocks placed dry in wide foundation trenches.

The building (**12**) now lies partly beneath the modern road (the old A27) and partly beneath houses and farm buildings on either side, but trial trenches dug in the gardens during the winter months when the flowers had died off and rather more extensive excavation in the old farmyard have revealed the main outlines of the building. Originally it covered an area of 190ft by more than 150ft and was composed of four main elements: a large colonnaded garden, a bath suite, and two ranges of rooms, one lying to the east of the courtyard and the other to the west of the baths.

The garden, which lay on the north side, was enclosed on at least three sides, and possibly on the fourth, by a veranda which on the west and north was double. Although only the footings survive, it is probable that it was provided with a colonnade on the garden side based on a ground-level stylobate (a foundation of large stone blocks). A

41

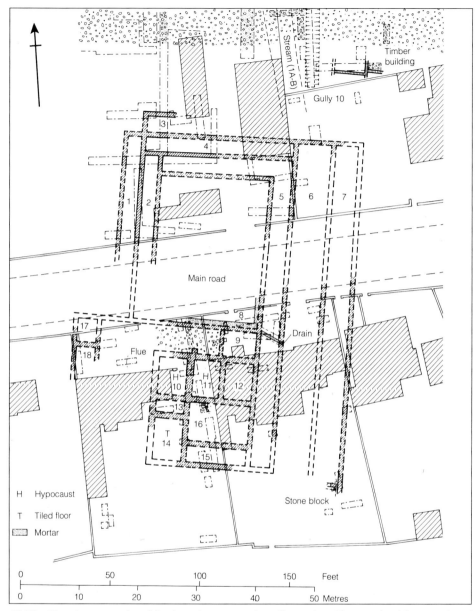

12 The Neronian proto-palace. Note how the reconstruction relies on the evidence produced by a number of small trial trenches

number of fragments of column drums made from greensand have been found belonging to this early period. Several of them have a roughened surface which might imply that they were originally furnished with a surfacing of stucco. Indeed this is likely because the greensand, if exposed to weathering, would have flaked very badly. Other columns seem to have been built up with quadrant or semicircular tiles and segments of stone mortared together and coated with stucco.

The proto-palace and its context

13 An ornate Corinthian capital reconstructed from fragments found reused as packing stones for posts in the Flavian garden. The columns were probably once incorporated in the garden or building of the proto-palace. The style is unusually elaborate for such an early period

When the garden of the main Flavian palace was being excavated, a large number of pieces of carved stone were found, used as packing for posts set up in the garden. These fragments clearly belonged to an earlier structure, but it was not for some time after jigsaw-puzzling the pieces together that we realized that they were the excrescences knocked off very ornate Corinthian capitals (**13**). These Corinthian capitals were very probably derived from the proto-palace and may well have been used somewhere in the garden, if not on the actual garden colonnades. The carving of the capitals is very lively and quite accomplished with elaborate ram's horn volutes projecting from each corner, faces wreathed in oak leaves between them and luxurious foliage below. It is surprising to find so much variety and assurance in carving at such an early date in the provinces, but parallels to most of the elements can be found in first-century work in Italy. Their

43

very existence at Fishbourne must imply the presence of continental craftsmen.

It seems probable that the living rooms were laid out in a single range of nearly 200ft along the veranda flanking the east side of the garden. Although the main walls have been defined, excavation has been so limited that practically nothing of the interiors or even the sizes of the individual rooms is known, but originally they must have been very elaborately decorated. Some evidence for this comes from the layers of rubble derived from the superstructure of the building when, a few years later, it was drastically modified and new floors inserted at a much higher level. The rubble consists of the remains of destroyed walls of wattle and daub which had been thickly plastered and painted. They were probably the partition walls of the rooms dismantled during the alterations. The painted plaster, though now broken into fragments, gives a very clear idea of the high standard of interior decoration. Basically the walls were divided into three zones, a lower dado about 3ft high, then the main wall panels, topped by a painted cornice, and finally a plain white frieze. The dado was painted with a dark blue-black background over which leaves and flowers were sketched with bold brush strokes of green, yellow and white. Above the dado the wall was divided into rectangular panels painted red, yellow and deep blue, enclosed in a plain white frame line and enlivened with another, coloured, frame line, usually about 2in in from the edge, yellow on the deep blue, white on the red and brown on the yellow. These panels were painted on a bright blue-green background which was allowed to appear in wide strips around them over-painted with elegant stylized floral designs in white with the occasional use of red and yellow (**Col 9**). The cornice, which capped the panels, was an accomplished piece of perspective painting giving the impression of a delicate moulding seen in the warm light of evening. While most of the painted fragments fall within this general range, other pieces in purples and ochres are known.

Some of the walls were visually divided by fluted pilasters made from stucco, an arrangement popular in Italy in the first century but so far unknown in Britain. The painting as well as the stucco work is of an extremely high standard; it is most unlikely that any native in Britain was skilled in these arts at such an early date. Again, therefore, it is necessary to suppose that foreign craftsmen were brought in.

No primary floors have been found in position in this part of the proto-palace, but the activity of the masons and their waste material mentioned above gives a good idea of what the floors were originally like. Apart from plain mortar, two finishes were in use: normal mosaic work using black and white *tesserae* and *opus sectile*. This entailed the construction of elaborate patterns from geometric shapes of coloured stone, here mainly red, blue and white with some grey and yellow (**Col 12**). Opus sectile floors were widespread in Italy and southern Gaul, but as a decorative technique it does not seem to have appealed to the Romano-Britons since very few examples are known in this country.

The third structural element of the proto-palace was the bath block which lay to the south of the courtyard. It was simple but effective, consisting of two separate parts: a cold swimming bath and a suite of heated rooms, joined only by a heated ante-room (no. 9), which probably served as an entrance chamber as well. The swimming bath only just projects into the area available for excavation; the rest of it now lies beneath the main road. All that survives is the corner, showing a bench of masonry, rendered with pink mortar, built around the wall of the room; the floor, which was probably of pink mortar as well, has been destroyed, but the outfall drain which led the waste water away shows that the bath must have been at least 3ft deep.

The heated suite is more complex, consisting of at least seven rooms, of which four (nos 10-12, 16) were heated by means of hypocausts from stoking chambers on the north or west side of the block. The three rooms closest to the heat source (nos 10-12) were probably *caldaria*, rooms of intense heat where the occupant would have sweated profusely in the steamy atmosphere, scraping his or her skin clean with a strigil. In all probability the rooms were heated to different temperatures and at least one of them may originally have been fitted with a hot bath provided with scalding water from a boiler built over one of the stokeries. None of these details, however, survive. Attached to the centre *caldarium* was a large rectangular room (no. 16) of somewhat gentler heat (the *tepidarium*). Part of its sub-floor structure survives, showing the emplacement of a semicircular plunge bath built against its north wall. The bathers could either rest in the warm atmosphere of the room or dip into the tepid water of the bath.

The room which opened out at the south-west corner of the *tepidarium* (no. 14) was floored with tiles and there is some evidence to suggest that a tiled bench had been built against the north wall. Unfortunately further excavation was not possible here, but it may well have been the cold room (*frigidarium*). Of the other two rooms defined by the excavation, there is little to be said except that they probably served as corridors, but how the suite linked onto the main range cannot now be defined.

Although the excavation was necessarily limited to a few small trial trenches dug in the flower beds of attractively laid-out gardens, a great deal of the Roman ground plan has been recovered. The rooms, however, had all been extensively robbed of their building materials late in the Roman period and practically nothing of the superstructure survives. How the walls were jacketed with box-tiles to lead the hot air through, and how the rooms were roofed are problems to which no firm answers can ever be given. Nevertheless the footings of the heated part of the bath suite were far more substantial than those in other parts of the proto-palace, a fact which implies that they were capable of supporting a much greater weight, presumably that of the masonry vaults with which the baths were probably roofed. Masonry vaulting had several advantages over timber in these contexts: it would not warp in the steamy atmosphere, it retained the heat more efficiently and it considerably reduced the risk of fire. We may tentatively assume, therefore, that the baths were vaulted, perhaps with two parallel east–west tunnels built of hollow box-tiles and concrete. A few fragments of voussoir-shaped box-tiles found in the destruction rubble add support to the view. It is difficult to know how the baths would have looked from the outside. If the well-preserved Hunting Baths at Lepcis Magna offer a guide, we must suppose that the vaults were left uncovered as bare concrete, but in a British climate it may have been necessary to clothe the masonry beneath a protective pitched roof of tiles.

The fourth part of the proto-palace is a group of rooms, of which only two are known, lying to the west of the baths and extending into an unexcavated area. Positive identification is impossible. While they may have been servants' quarters, tucked out of sight but conveniently linked by passageways to the main building and close to the stoking chambers of the baths, it is more likely that they formed the eastern extremity of a residential range later incorporated into the Southern Wing of the Flavian palace.

In the context of what had gone before at Fishbourne, the proto-palace was architecturally a great advance, its very structure implying the attentions of a large number of foreign specialists well versed in constructional and decorative arts. When functions and residential space are considered, however, it is not so dissimilar to the earlier timber house. The main range of rooms with its fronting veranda is repeated in both, and both have room for servants. The difference lies in the addition of luxuries such as the colonnaded courtyard and the baths. It is the very existence of these purely Roman luxuries, together with the quality of the internal decoration, which underlines the change in status between the two buildings. It is probably correct to consider them together because the proto-palace does seem to replace the timber house in so far as the timber buildings were still standing while the shell of the proto-palace was being erected, and were not demolished until the time had come for the final decorative touches to be added. The progression from one to the other could simply reflect a change in the wealth and status of the owning family, but these points must be reserved for later discussion.

The proto-palace is not unique even in Sussex, for only 16 miles to the east, at Angmering, part of a closely similar building has been excavated, incorporating many of the same architectural skills and evidently drawing on the same sources of supply for the raw materials. The tiles used in the two buildings are identical and Angmering has produced a number of *opus sectile* elements similar in material and shape to those from Fishbourne. The parallels are so close that the two buildings must surely have been constructed largely by the same labour force. There must have been many aristocrats in the area only too ready to invest capital in these expensive Roman luxuries, now that Roman government was so clearly here to stay. The Roman villas at Southwick, Wiggonholt and Pulborough all have interesting peculiarities in their designs which set them apart from the normal Romano-British villa development. Perhaps they, too, were begun in this early period.

The proto-palace was not the only masonry building of pre-Flavian date to be found at Fishbourne. Two others are known (11): Building M1 occupied the higher ground to the west and was partially covered by the West Wing of the Flavian palace while Building M3 was discovered in 1983 in the field to the east of the palace and has since been totally excavated.

Building M1 is something of a puzzle. It was evidently designed to be a structure of some importance but it was never completed above foundation level: instead a stone-built culvert was cut through two of the footings and the site was left open until the West Wing was constructed across part of it. The plan, as we at present have it, is partial but the known foundations appear to comprise the east end of a much larger complex. A number of ranges of rooms and corridors can be defined but excavation has been selective and not all of the walls have been identified. This, combined with the absence of floors, makes it impossible to suggest how the building might have been intended to function but one possibility is that the large square room in the centre of the east side may have been designed as an entrance hall. It lay on the axis of the southern road with which the building was exactly aligned. The nature and extent of Building M1 presents an intriguing problem which may one day be resolved by further excavation.

Building M3 is equally enigmatic. Its plan, now largely known, shows it to have been symmetrically planned about an east–west axis. A large 'courtyard' flanked by corridors to the north and south occupied the central part with rooms at either end. One interpretation would be to see the eastern room as comprising a hall opening on to the courtyard with the main entrance opposite in the west range but other interpretations are equally possible and until the excavations have been completed it is best to leave the matter open. The foundations, consisting of layers of flint nodules up to a metre deep, were certainly substantial enough to have taken a masonry superstructure.

Building M3 is dated to the period c. AD 60–70 and may therefore be contemporary with the timber buildings to the west or the proto-palace. That it may have begun before work began on the proto-palace is suggested by the fact that the northern road, which we believe to have been remetalled when the proto-palace was being built, ran across the northern extension of the west wall of the building. Clearly the sequence is complex but is likely to be resolved by the current excavation.

Sufficient will have been said to show that in the decade or so before the palace was built, that is c. AD 65–75, three extraordinary masonry buildings were constructed at Fishbourne. Clearly the site was the focus of an unusual burst of energy but what it all means is far from clear. It could be argued that the buildings were part of a commercial settlement developing at the head of the harbour and that the proto-palace was nothing more than a public bath suite put up to serve the community. In this interpretation the eastern part of the building, which we have suggested is a residential range, could be explained away as an aisled exercise hall. But against this the exceptionally high quality of the decorative finishes and the fact that the building was incorporated into the Flavian palace argue that it was a private complex belonging to a person of some wealth. He or his heirs were influential enough, a few years later, to transform the site totally into a single huge palatial structure, sweeping away all the other buildings in their way. Could it be that Buildings M1 and M3 represent the first stages of an abortive attempt to monumentalize the site, left unfinished for some reason, later to be eclipsed by an even more grandiose scheme? These intriguing possibilities can be addressed only by further excavation.

6. The building of the Flavian Palace

It was some time between AD 75 and 80 that the construction of the great palace began, a few years after Vespasian became emperor in 69, founding the Flavian dynasty. The dating of the initial stages of the building depends upon the pottery and coins found sealed in and beneath its floor levels. A relatively large collection of coins, including issues of the early part of Vespasian's reign (but none dating after the year 73) were found below the floors. Clearly, then, building cannot have begun before 73 but, judging by the relatively unworn state of the latest issues, it must have started soon after, before the coins had been long in circulation. The imported samian pottery from beneath the floor levels is similarly helpful: the latest vessels, large, highly decorated bowls, were made in the same Gaulish factories as an important group found in one of the shops in Pompeii buried by the eruption of Vesuvius in AD 79. These vessels therefore support the dating of the coins and indicate that the main building activity at Fishbourne took place in the second half of the 70s. The very latest of the construction levels of the palace, the garden surfaces and the upper metalling of the service road, produced two coins of Vespasian's successor, Domitian, suggesting that the finishing touches were being made to the palace in the 80s. The whole project, then, must have taken at least five years to complete, which is hardly surprising considering its enormous size.

The architects, who first surveyed the site, were faced with a problem: the land sloped down to the old filled-in stream bed, from about 26ft Ordnance Datum at the west to 15ft OD at the lowest point. It also sloped to the south towards the harbour. In spite of the digging of a number of drainage gullies in the preceding period and the rerouting of the stream, the low-lying areas were still damp and ill-drained. The solution was simple — a complete levelling of the entire site (**14**). In practice this meant that the western part of the site was left at its original level of 25ft OD, and a vast artificial terrace was created to the east at a height of about 20ft OD, covering an area of 400ft by 900ft. Altogether more than 36,000 cubic yards of clay and gravel were removed from the west part of the area and dumped over the eastern part.

The actual progress of the work was of course more complicated. For example, to cover the eastern part of the site with 5ft of clay and gravel and then to attempt to put up a building on it would have been structurally ill-advised. What in practice the Roman builders did was to dig the foundation trenches first, throwing the spoil out into the

14 The present day village of New Fishbourne with the area of the first-century Roman palace buildings cross hatched. Compare its size to the size of houses of the eighteenth to twentieth century

areas between the walls, and then to lay their concrete footings. When these had set they began to build the free-standing part of the ashlar superstructure, allowing splashes of mortar and chippings from the tooling of the blocks to accumulate in heaps within the rooms. Only after this stage had been completed were the clay and rubble brought in from outside and spread around, up to the required level. The saving in time and labour allowed by this simple piece of forward planning was enormous. Problems arose with the existing proto-palace because its floor levels related to the original ground surface and not the newly created one, but these were simply overcome by disregarding all earlier floors and raising the entire level of the old building, using the remains of its demolished wattle and daub walls in the levelling process.

The acquisition of the building materials needed for the entire complex was a significant feat of organization. To give some idea of what was involved, we must

The building of the Flavian Palace

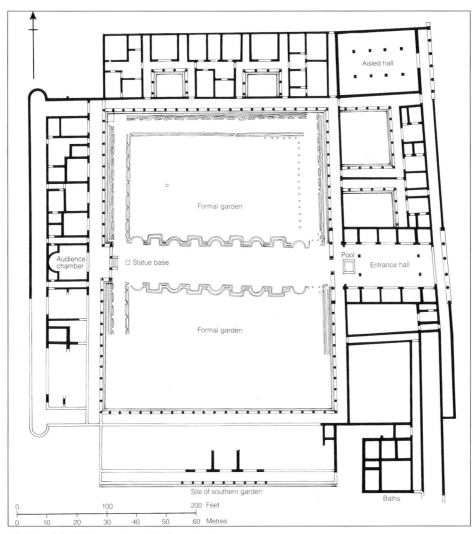

15 Plan of the Flavian palace and its formal garden

consider a single stretch of wall. First of all a foundation trench was dug into the solid clay, some 2½ ft wide and of about the same depth. Into the bottom of this pairs of oak piles, 3ft long and about 6in in diameter, were rammed every foot, so that the walls of a single average-sized room would have needed between 150 and 200 piles. The foundation trenches were then filled with flints set in concrete and above this the superstructure, consisting of walls 1½–2ft thick built of squared greensand blocks, was erected to the full height of the single-storied building. In all some two miles of walling was built in this way.

Two types of basic building stone were used, greensand and Mixon limestone. The greensand, geologically Upper Greensand from below the chalk, probably came from the Weald near Pulborough, conveniently close for Stane Street to provide easy road transport. This type of stone was used for all but the West Wing of the palace which was built of blocks of a coarse limestone, from the Mixon reef off Selsey Bill, many of them water-eroded slabs collected from near the tide level.

All the gardens of the palace were surrounded by colonnades based on a foundation of large stone blocks, called a stylobate, and fronted by a continuous ground-level stone gutter. The structural and visual implications of these colonnades will be considered later – here we are concerned with the stone. The gutter blocks, each about 3ft wide, 4ft long and 2ft thick, were of two different stones: a greenish sandstone of a type found in a reef off Bracklesham, a few miles south of Chichester, and a fossiliferous limestone outcropping in the cliffs at Bembridge in the Isle of Wight. The stylobate blocks were all of Bembridge limestone. It is interesting that both outcrops should be close to the sea: sea transport was easy and cheap and Fishbourne with its harbour was ideally suited to be supplied by boat.

The columns, of which there were more than 160, were made from various limestones including an oolitic stone from Gloucestershire and Caen stone from Northern France. Such wide-flung connections show that the masons were in a position to choose carefully the stone most suited to the job.

The roofing of the building would have required colossal quantities of timber, presumably cut in the nearby oak forests of the coastal plain, as well as many tons of iron nails. The roof covering was of the standard *imbrex* and *tegulae* tiles, probably made at Dell Quay, two miles to the south on the edge of the Fishbourne inlet, where extensive remains of Roman tile production have come to light. Finally, many hundreds of tons of lime-mortar were used, made by burning chalk from the nearby Downs and mixing the lime thus formed with a pebbly flint aggregate derived from the gravel deposits east of Chichester.

For the basic structure alone the problem of shipping correct quantities of materials at the right stage of the building programme must have been enormous, not least because many of the sources were being exploited for the first time, presumably by native labour quite unused to building in masonry. The logistics of man management alone would have been enough to frighten many a modern clerk of works into a nervous decline.

Governing all these issues of the supply of materials and of labour was the basic plan to which the architects were working. The palace was to consist of four residential ranges arranged around a large central garden 250ft by 320ft, while to the south was to be a second garden of comparable size leading down to the sea (**15**). The building faced east towards Chichester, to which it was linked by the existing southern road, belonging initially to the military period. To the west, behind the main palace, were to be the servants' quarters and other domestic installations. Everything was well thought out and planned in advance. While different phases in the building programme can be distinguished, the entire concept is evidently of one period, excepting of course the earlier proto-palace which was incorporated into the south-east corner.

The basic principles behind the design were simple. A central east–west axis was created projecting the line of the road, and astride this, in the East Wing, the entrance hall was built. The axis was continued across the garden as a hedge-lined path and ended in front of the audience chamber built in the centre of the West Wing. About this axis the building was arranged as symmetrically as possible. The entrance hall, garden and West Wing functioned as a single unit, all three elements being in easy visual and

The West Wing

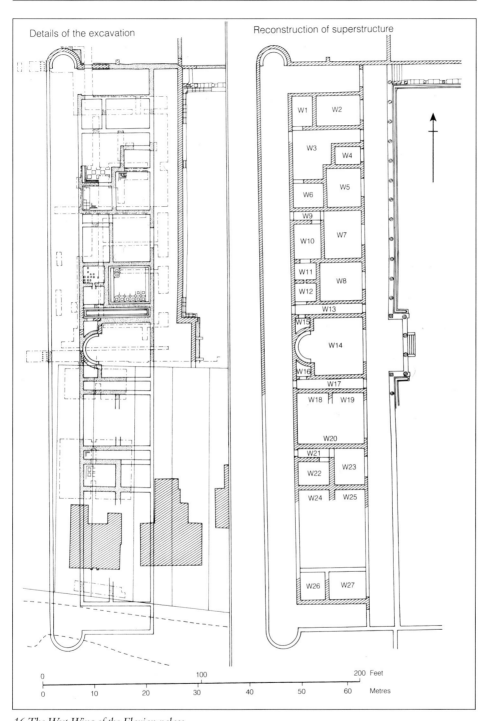

16 *The West Wing of the Flavian palace*

physical communication and linked to the outside world, whilst the North and South Wings and the remaining parts of the East Wing were essentially private environments in-turned upon themselves.

The West Wing

The West Wing (**16**) was the visual and functional centrepiece of the design. It was the first part of the building to be seen in its entirety by a visitor, and it was here that the principal administrative rooms lay. The wing was given an added grandeur by being built on the upper (25ft OD) terrace while the ground level of the garden and the rest of the palace in front of it was 5ft lower. The change in level was revetted by a masonry wall, the top of which served to support the stylobate for the fronting colonnade on a level with the West Wing floors. Behind this colonnade, more than 330ft long, lay the range of rooms, of which the northern half has been extensively excavated and the southern half sampled. There would originally have been about 27 rooms. Unfortunately, the height of the floor levels, and the corresponding shallow soil coverage which accumulated over them after the Roman period, has meant that they have suffered very considerably from post-Roman agricultural activities, particularly the ploughing of the late Saxon and early medieval periods. In many instances the floors and the concrete make-up beneath them have been scoured away by ploughing, but in spite of the destruction a remarkable amount of structural and decorative detail still survives (**Col 13**).

The principal room in the wing lay exactly on the centre axis: it was a large square chamber 31ft by 35ft with an apsidal recess 20ft in diameter opening out of its west wall (**17**). From its position and structure there can be little doubt that originally it served as an audience chamber, built in contemporary Italian style which its architect was so carefully trying to imitate. Almost the entire floor had been destroyed by ploughing, including much of the concrete and rubble beneath it, but a few small patches of a mosaic pavement survived; in the corner of the apse an area showing a black border with a leaf inside it remained in position and further towards the centre of the room were two smaller areas depicting a twisted guilloche design laid in white, black, yellow and red. The quality of the work was exceptionally fine with individual *tesserae* $\frac{1}{8} - \frac{1}{10}$ in square laid very tightly and carefully together. Nowhere in the rest of the palace is there evidence of such exquisite craftsmanship. The master mosaicist must have given the audience chamber his personal attention.

The interior fittings of the room would have been largely movable, and of these there is no trace, but in the apse the impression made by a timber bench was found lining the curved wall. In such a prominent position, where the owner would have sat in state, we must imagine a structure upholstered in high quality but nothing now survives apart from its bare impression. We have, then, the ground plan of the room and some traces of the interior layout, but it is also possible to reconstruct the basic superstructure and to think of the room in terms of its volume and carefully contrived visual effects (**18**). To begin with, the fronting colonnade gave way to a projecting platform in front of the room. This would have taken an impressive pedimented front supported on four large columns. The spacing of the columns elsewhere, and the general proportions which can

17 Architectural reconstruction of the audience chamber (after a drawing by Nigel Sunter)

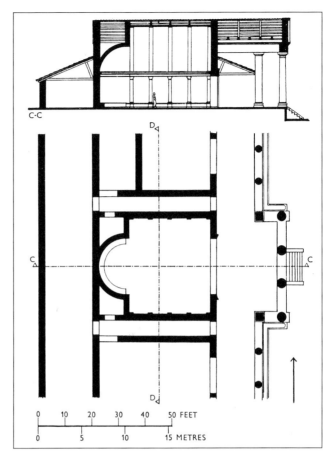

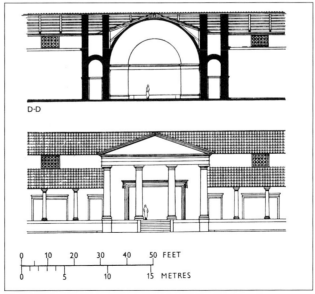

18 The audience chamber in the centre of the West Wing. The apsidal recess can be clearly seen; it had once been lined by a timber bench. The mosaic floor has almost entirely disappeared, except for a small patch in the corner. The proximity of modern gardens unfortunately prevents further excavation

be deduced from them, demand a tetrastyle treatment. The higher floor of the West Wing was reached, from the garden level (**19**), by a flight of wooden steps retained by side walls which exactly relate to the space between the two centre columns.

From the columns preserved in position in the north-west corner of the garden, we know that the height of the veranda architrave would have been about 12ft which, allowing for a sloping veranda roof and provision for windows above this in the main range to allow light into the rooms, would have meant that the eaves of the range were at about 25ft above the floor. Since this is almost exactly the height to which the four big columns supporting the pediment should have stood, the implication is that the audience chamber and the main range were roofed at the same height. These somewhat confusing calculations are more clearly expressed in the simple elevation reconstruction.

The most satisfactory way to have roofed the audience chamber would have been by means of a vault with its haunches resting on the north and south walls. Such an arrangement would have focused attention on the apsidal recess, itself roofed with a semi-dome, and at the same time it would have created feelings of space which a flat ceiling would not. Evidence for the vaulted ceiling is provided by the recovery of a number of fragments of stucco from the room showing raised ribs picked out in white against a background of bright blue, purple and red. Some of the pieces have a slight curve, strongly suggesting that they came from a vault which may well have been

The West Wing

19 In front of the audience chamber the revetting wall, which retained the higher platform of the West Wing, was brought forward to form a porch area reached by a flight of steps. The wall was of flint and mortar faced with limestone blocks and rendered with mortar. At ground level were the massive blocks of the gutter

constructed of a timber to which a plaster rendering was applied.

Audience chambers of this kind are known in the Mediterranean world, the closest near-contemporary example being in the famous palace of Domitian on the Palatine in Rome. It has been suggested that the huge soaring vault of the roof and the semi-domed recess in which the emperor would have sat in state are an attempt to capture in masonry the feeling of a god sitting in heaven. It is perhaps significant that the idea of the apsidal-ended audience chamber seems to have been the model for the earliest forms of Christian church!

The Fishbourne audience chamber lay in the centre of a long range of rooms but it was divided from them by flanking corridors which served as a convenient means of access from one side of the building to the other (**20**), and at the same time helped to isolate the room from the noise of the rest of the building. The rooms to the north seem to have been planned as two blocks, numbers W1–6 forming one and W7–12 the other. In the northern block room W3 served as a general concourse from which access to the other rooms was probably provided, but only one doorway leading to room W6 has survived the extensive destruction. All of the rooms were originally floored with black and white mosaic pavements but those in rooms W1, 2, and 4 have been almost totally destroyed. In room W3, however, a substantial area survives of a complex pattern of square panels linked with areas of a Greek key pattern which also spread into the areas between the panels (**21–2**). The panels are filled with a variety of geometric motifs. This

20 The mosaic floor of corridor W13. The centre had been worn and was patched with areas of pink mortar

general type of arrangement was very popular in Italy in the first century AD and can be paralleled on many of the early sites in Rome and at Herculaneum and Pompeii. The same type of pattern was used again at Fishbourne in room N13 in the centre of the North Wing.

The mosaic in room W6 incorporated totally different ideas. It was divided into two parts: a 'mat' of chequer pattern along the west wall and the main 'carpet' filling the rest of the room (**23**). The division was made so that a person entering through the door in the north-west corner would walk out onto the mat and would be able to obtain a clear view of the entire carpet. Sadly, very little of the carpet area has survived except for its border of black triangles arranged base to apex, but there may have been a figured design in the centre —we will never know. Of the mosaic in room W5 only a small corner now remains showing a bordering panel of tendrils, about 2ft wide, which would have run the full length of the room, possibly balanced by a similar panel on the opposite side of the room, as was the case with room W8. Although the floor was largely a black-on-white design, the node of the tendril which survived was picked out in yellow. If the simple arrangement here was like that in room W8, then the nodes would have alternated red and yellow.

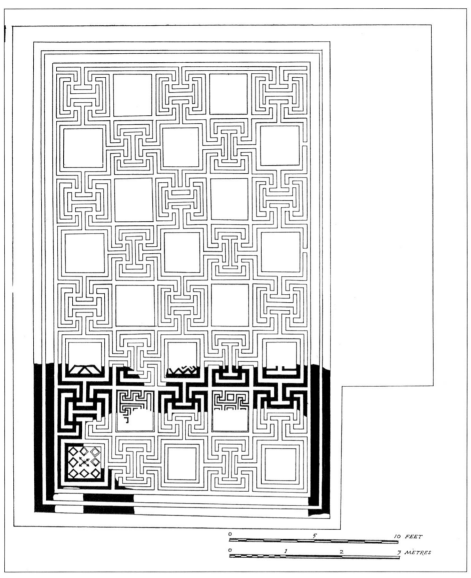

21 The Flavian mosaic in room W3. Reconstruction of the original design

The cold all-over black and white of the floors contrasted sharply with the rich bright colours with which the walls were painted. From the surviving pieces of wall plaster it appears that the walls of room W3 were painted as an area of composite mock marble inlay, one of a blue-grey colour given a vague texture by smearing with a wide brush, another next to it was basically purple deliberately splashed with red and white to give a speckled appearance. These two areas were divided from each other by black and white lines meant to represent a simple moulding. These 'marble sheets' probably formed the dado above which would have been areas painted in plain bright colours. Evidence of the decor of room W6 also survived. Here there were areas of pink overpainted with

The building of the Flavian Palace

22 *The Flavian mosaic in room W3 showing the strip that survived below a later wall and a small patch remaining in the corner patched in one place with coarse red tesserae*

23 The Flavian mosaic in room W6 showing the only surviving part

bold purple designs together with areas of red, pale blue and purple.

The second set of rooms, numbers W7–12, were rather differently arranged: two big rooms, W7 and 8, fronted directly onto the veranda and were entered through wide east-facing doorways. These were clearly important state apartments second only to the audience chamber. Behind them were four other rooms, all floored with pink mortar. Room W9 served as a corridor leading from W7 to the back of the building and incidentally giving access to room W10 through various doors, the timber sills of two of which have survived. Room W10 was a simple unadorned room out of which opened the smaller W11, the floor of which was heated by a hypocaust, the only example of central heating in the Flavian palace outside the bath block. The stoking chamber for the hypocaust was provided in room W12, which could be entered only from the corridor to the south. This back range with its heated room is an interesting feature, but not immediately easy to explain. One possibility, however, is that the rooms formed a suite to which guests might retire during a chilly evening: the front rooms would have caught the sun all day but the west-facing side would have benefited only from the weaker evening sun — perhaps some booster heat was required.

Rooms W7 and 8 were probably both floored with mosaics, but the floor of room W7 has been totally destroyed. In W8, however, substantial areas of mosaic work remain (**24–5; Col 6**). The main design, in black and white, was a highly repetitive arrangement of the box-within-box pattern which was so popular in the Roman world. On either side of it were long tendril panels drawn in black, yellow and red, on a white background. The relatively dull all-over pattern would have been acceptable in a room frequently used and perhaps partly obscured by furniture. Unlike the floor in W6 it was not constructed to impress visitors.

The building of the Flavian Palace

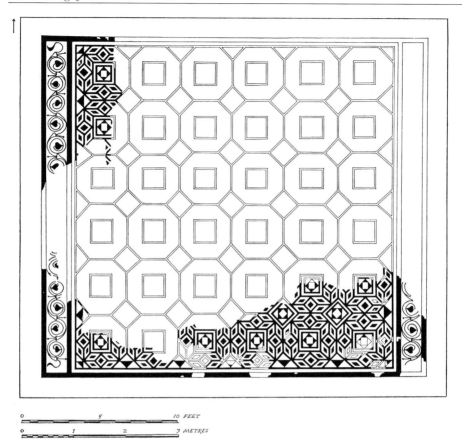

24 The Flavian mosaic in room W8 of the West Wing. Reconstruction of the original design

The room with the heated floor, room W11, produced sufficient painted wall plaster to show that its walls were rendered with pink mortar which was painted in areas of plain red and plain white adjacent to each other, with the junction between the colours overpainted with a thin black line. The red probably came from the dado while the wall above was simply painted white. It seems that somewhere in the room, just below the ceiling, over the door or perhaps framing a window or recess, an elaborate cornice had been painted and elsewhere in the decor there were areas of bright blue-green.

The two small alcoves behind the audience chamber were floored with white mortar: they were probably nothing more than store rooms leading out of the flanking corridors. But both corridors were an essential part of the stylish range, for they were floored with a very simple black and white mosaic in which the central white panel was carefully constructed of tesserae laid diagonally to the borders (**20**).

The southern part of the West Wing lies between modern houses and gardens. That some floors remained was, however, demonstrated by the discovery of a fragment of black and white mosaic floor uncovered by children in 1938. In 1987–8 the opportunity arose to excavate in two of the gardens with the result that part of the plan of the southern part of the wing was recovered. Although destruction had been extensive several fragments of black and white mosaic were recorded. Of these the largest, from

25 The Flavian mosaic in room W8. Much of the centre had been worn away allowing an exploratory excavation of the layers and features beneath it

room W22, was composed of a grid of panels each containing contrasting geometric patterns (**26**). The corridor, room W21, was floored in the same plain style of the two corridors flanking the audience chamber. Sufficient of the overall plan was recovered to show that the two halves of the wing were not symmetrically arranged.

The main range of rooms, comprising the West Wing, was surrounded by wide verandas and, as we have suggested, the east veranda was colonnaded so that the rooms facing east had a clear view of the garden. The nature of the colonnades will be considered separately in the next chapter. How the western corridor was treated is much less clear: in plan it was 17ft wide and ran the entire length of the wing, finishing at its north end, and presumably also the south, with a large apsidal recess lined originally with a stone-built bench. This much is clear but its width is excessive for a simple service corridor and unlike the east-facing veranda with its colonnade forming an important visual part of the great garden, there is no reason to suppose the existence of a west-facing colonnade, nor is there any evidence for gardens to the west requiring a colonnade of this kind. One explanation, however, might be that the corridor served as an exercise space, a hippodromos, in which one might play games or run from end to end pausing to rest in the alcoves. A closely similar arrangement is known in Domitian's palace and is by no means uncommon in other early Roman villas in Italy. If this were so, the west wall might have been perforated with large windows or even provided with balustrades so that the evening light could reach the interior.

The corridor was decorated in the same style throughout with a dado of pink splashed

The building of the Flavian Palace

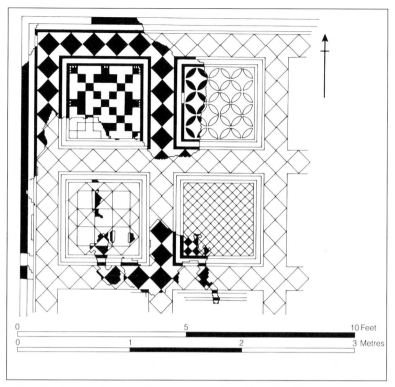

26 The Flavian mosaic in room W22. Reconstruction of the original design

with black, white and ochre to imitate a coarse-grained marble: at the base of the dado was a narrow deep red skirting. The main walls above the dado level were painted white marked out in panels bordered by deep red bands, and concentric with the red borders were thin black frame lines. The apse was picked out for a more specialized treatment. Here the wall panels were yellow with a thin brown frame line. The colours were deliberately kept simple and light as would befit an area set aside for gentle exercise and relaxation.

From the foregoing description it would appear that the West Wing was laid out to dominate the great garden which lay in front of it. With its central pedimented front supported on four large columns and reached by a flight of steps, it was designed to impress but at the same time it was essentially an extension of the garden environment — a visitor walking in the garden had direct access to all its main rooms. This 'semi-public' aspect of the plan supports the idea that the audience chamber and the flanking state rooms were the administrative and official chambers. As we shall see, the other wings were conceived in a totally different way.

The North Wing

The North Wing (**27**) lay in a single block, measuring some 70ft by 255ft, across the north side of the garden. Its 23 rooms were arranged rather like a letter E, the spaces

1 General view across the military store building north of the northern road. The structure of the building was supported on a grid of posts placed at 8ft intervals in large rectangular pits. The voids of two of the original timbers can be seen

2 The bridge by which the northern road crossed the stream. The western abutment, shown here, was constructed of a row of revetting posts, taking the main span of the bridge with a causeway of rubble and gravel leading out to it

3 General view across the North Wing of the palace during excavation looking west. The room with the Cupid mosaic is centre right

4 General view across the North Wing of the palace looking east

5 The Flavian mosaic in room N20 showing part of the border of the central roundel

6 The Flavian mosaic in room W7 showing a detail of the border

7 The Flavian mosaic in room N21. One of the few coloured mosaics in the first-century palace. The small white diamond in the border to the left may be the mosaicist's signature. The floor has slumped into the soft fillings of earlier features below

8 Part of a frieze of moulded stucco from the North Wing of the palace. The design is repetitive, showing two birds with fruit in their beaks standing on either side of vases of fruit (see 33). The moulding probably came from the junction of wall and ceiling

9 Fragment of painted wall plaster from the proto-palace showing a floral motif on a vertical border flanking a panel painted to represent yellow marble

10 Fragment of a Roman wall painting dating to the early Flavian period. It shows a colonnaded villa against the background of the sea. An almost identical painting was found at Stabiae in Italy destroyed during the eruption of Vesuvius in AD 79

11 Elements of different coloured marbles once used to ornament a wall seen here where they had fallen onto a tessellated floor when the building was destroyed by fire in the late third century

12 Opus sectile elements. Quantities of these shapes of coloured stone were found in levels contemporary with the Neronian proto-palace. They would have been used largely for floor decoration. The elements here are arranged in patterns, based on those found at Pompeii and Herculaneum

13 Part of the West Wing seen from the apse of the audience chamber, looking north. Very little of the superstructure of the walls has survived the robbing and ploughing to which the area was subjected in Saxon and medieval times

14 View across the centre of the formal garden, showing the bedding trenches for hedges cut into the gravel. The diagonal rubble features are recent drains and the pond in the centre of the trench is modern

15 General view of the replanted garden as it is now, taken from approximately the same position as Col 14, but 30 years later. Box bushes have been planted over the original Roman bedding trenches and a tree now stands in the position in which a bedding pit was discovered

16 The garden paths lined by bedding trenches in the north-west corner of the formal garden

17 The extreme north-west corner of the garden showing the stylobate of the northern veranda and one of its displaced columns. The masonry structure is the base of a water tank which once served the garden fountain

18 Part of the colonnade and stylobate on the north side of the formal garden

19 The Cupid mosaic in room N7

20 Sea panther from the Cupid mosaic

21 Central roundel from the Cupid mosaic

22 The first-century mosaic in room N13 was replaced by a polychrome floor about AD 100. The earlier floor can be seen in patches through holes in the later

23 Second-century mosaic in room N5. The floor may depict a peacock of which only two ill-formed legs and its splayed tail survive

24 Second-century mosaic in the southern half of room N11

25 Third-century mosaic in the southern part of room N8

26 The channelled hypocaust system inserted into room N1 in the late third century just before the fire which destroyed the building. The system was never completed

The North Wing

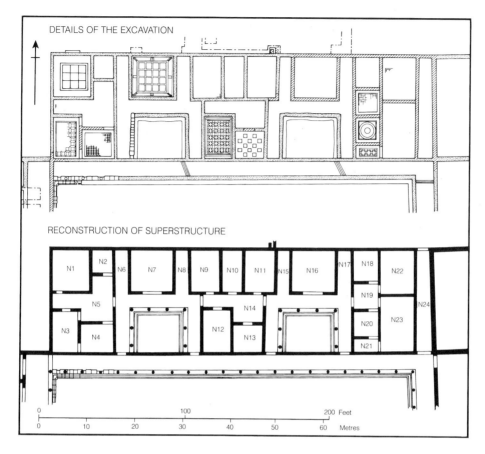

27 The North Wing of the Flavian palace

between the short arms being occupied by small private gardens surrounded on three sides by colonnades and closed on the fourth with a blank wall (**Col 3–4**). The whole wing seems to have been designed as a group of two or three private suites turned in upon their own gardens to provide luxury and peace. The first suite, comprising rooms N1–5, is not unlike the northern part of the West Wing in plan. It is essentially four rooms opening out of a general concourse (N5) which seems to have been floored with a simple black and white mosaic. Room N1, the largest in the suite, was provided with a complex mosaic floor, a small part of which now survives showing it to consist of a rigid geometric pattern of squares-within-squares picked out in black with the limited use of red and blue (**28**).

Room N2 had been so altered in later times that nothing of the original Flavian decoration survived but the floors of rooms N3 and 4 remained virtually intact, apart from some holes which were allowed to wear in them when the rooms were later given over to domestic functions. The positions of the original door sills show that, in addition to being entered direct from the concourse, they were interlinked by a door which at a later stage was walled up. The mosaic floor in room N3 (**29, 30**) was a relatively simple arrangement of square panels, linked together by a diamond-patterned

65

The building of the Flavian Palace

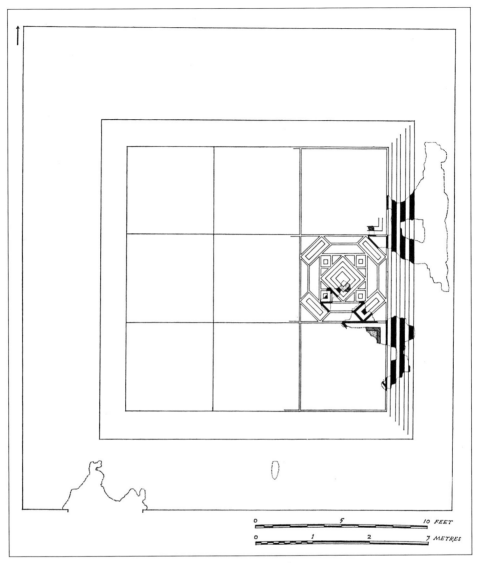

28 The Flavian mosaic in room N1. Reconstruction of the original design

border, and filled with one of three geometric motifs. The basic feeling was one of lightness and simplicity. In contrast the floor in room N4 consisted of a repetitive arrangement of black squares of two sizes on a white ground; here the impression is of darkness (**31–2**). The floors, of course, are only one part of the decorative design; to appreciate fully their effect it would be necessary to see them in relation to the wall and ceiling painting but unfortunately, in the case of rooms N3 and 4, nothing of the original painting scheme survives. Between the western suite and the central suite lay the simple colonnaded courtyard with a single large room, N7, fronting on to it. The room was flanked by two elongated rooms or corridors, rooms N6 and 8, both of which had been subjected to considerable later alteration leaving their original function far from clear.

29 The Flavian mosaic in room N3. Reconstruction of the original design

30 The Flavian mosaic in room N3. In the third century the room was used as a workshop and the floor was allowed to wear out. When excavated it was found to be covered by masses of charred rafters and broken roof tiles from the final conflagration

The North Wing

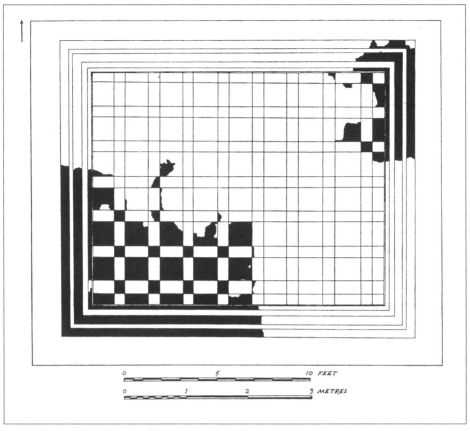

31 The Flavian mosaic in room N4. This room was also used as a workshop in the third century

While it is not totally impossible that they served as stairways to an upper storey, there is no other evidence to suggest more than one floor and moreover four stairways (rooms N6, 8, 15 and 17) would seem a little excessive. A more likely explanation is that they were used as service rooms in connection with dining, for which room N7 and its counterpart room N16 are so well designed. The original mosaic in room N7 was exposed in 1980 when the superimposed Dolphin mosaic was lifted for restoration. The design consists of a central panel surrounded by a wide border (**33**). The central panel was composed of sixteen squares each ornamented with a complex geometric pattern based on triangles and squares. Of the nine that survive, albeit only in fragments, there is no repetition suggesting that all sixteen may have been different. The surrounding border is a schematic representation of a crenellated city wall with towers in the corners and gates in the centres of the four sides enlivened in grey and red: two single portal and two double portal. Although unique in Britain, depictions of city walls are well known in mosaics of the first century in the western provinces. The mass of wall plaster recovered from the rubble filling the room is more likely to belong to the second-century phase of alterations and will accordingly be described later. From the north robber trench, however, came several pieces of two stucco mouldings which almost certainly belong to the original Flavian decor. The best-preserved depicts a simple frieze

The building of the Flavian Palace

32 General view across the west end of the North Wing of the palace showing rooms N3 and N4

of pairs of birds holding fruit in their beaks and standing on either side of a vase of fruit (**34; Col 8**). Sufficient survives to show that the design is repetitive and a careful examination of the join between one section and the next clearly demonstrates how each section was impressed onto the damp plaster, presumably with a wooden block. The simple cornice moulding above the frieze and the bead-and-reel below were probably also applied in this way.

The 'bird moulding' was of sufficient proportions to have occupied a position high on the wall, but the second moulding, a small section simply decorated in what is known as an egg-and-dart motif, probably comes from lower down on the walls, framing perhaps a recess set into a wall face. The discovery of moulded stucco is remarkable in Britain. It was a technique common enough in Italy but for some reason it did not seem to find wide favour in this country.

A considerable quantity of early wall plaster was recovered from the courtyard, coming from the faces of the walls which formed its west, north and east sides. The west wall and part at least of the north wall were painted with a pink and purple background which served as a basis for bold green and blue foliage painting. The east wall was, however, more restrained with a dado of painted mock marble slabs in varying tones of splashed and smeared purple and green, each divided from the next by simply painted vertical 'mouldings'. Above the dado came a band of red merging to yellow representing a simple cornice moulding, with bands of deep blue, bright green and red above. An exactly similar type of painting was also recovered from the north-west corner of the courtyard.

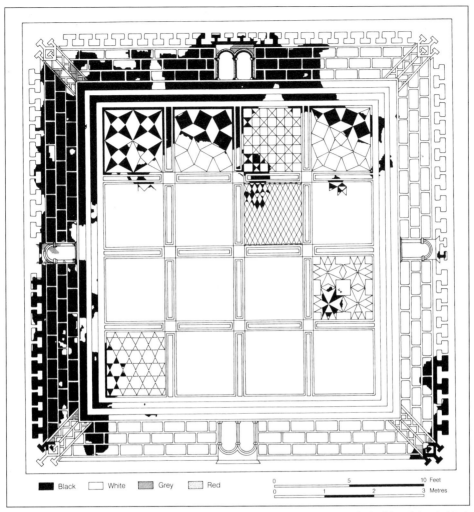

33 The Flavian mosaic in room N7 found when the Dolphin mosaic above it was lifted. Although largely black and white, details of the gates and corner towers are enhanced with grey and red tesserae

The central suite, rooms N9–13, was arranged around the L-shaped room N14 which formed a concourse as well as allowing free access between the two courtyards. Out of it must have opened doors leading to the five adjacent rooms. Traces of the original floor show that it was of mosaic with, in one area at least, the *tesserae* set in rows diagonally to the borders in the style of corridor W13. The black and white mosaic which now occupies the southern part of the room, though laid in the style of the early floors, can be shown to overlie part of the original mosaic and is therefore later. It may be, however, that in its present form it is simply a relaid version of the original using the same materials and copying the same design but with less craftsmanship. Alternatively it may be a copy of the early mosaic in room N12. At any event it is interesting that the later occupiers should want to retain the style of the Flavian decor.

A small area of wall plaster survived in position in the south-west corner of the room.

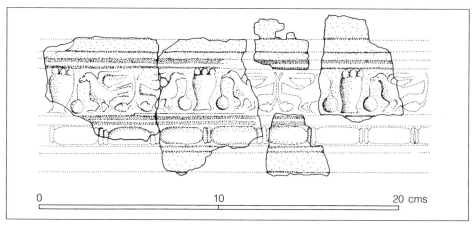

34 Fragments of a stucco moulding found in the North Wing: length 20 cm

It belonged to the dado which here was painted pink and splashed with blue and red with the joints between the marbled areas shown as a simple black line. Only 9in survived of the dado which would originally have been about 3ft high, but indications of the wall panels above are provided by fragments lying loose in the rubble, including areas painted in plain green, yellow, orange, red and blue with interior frame lines very much in the style of the wall painting of the proto-palace.

The three rooms which form the northern part of the middle suite (N9–11) were all refloored in the later period after most of the original mosaics had been ripped up. Now all that remains of the original floors is a few of the *tesserae* around the edges of the rooms and a small patch of mosaic in the south-east corner of room N9, comparable in style to the 'mat' already described in room W6 in the West Wing. The importance of these rooms lies in the remarkable state of preservation of the wall decoration, which probably dates back to the Flavian period. Room N9 yielded a large quantity of painted wall plaster, much of it in quite large pieces allowing a fairly full reconstruction of the design. Here, more than anywhere else in the palace, it is possible to appreciate the rich, almost overbearing, nature of the mock marble painting. Like most of the first-century designs the room was provided with a dado about 3ft high painted in imitation of large sheets of boldly veined pink and red marble, each sheet divided from the next by a vertical black line intended to represent the junction between the individual slabs. Above this was an elaborate horizontal cornice painted in stripes of black and white, to represent highlight and shadow, and a green merging to orange which resembles a gently curving moulding. Above the cornice the wall was divided into a series of rectangular panels capped by another cornice a foot or more below the ceiling height. The panels were of two types, the very elaborate representation of multicoloured inlaid marble and much simpler areas of speckled orange, or speckled deep blue to contrast with them and relieve their vividness. One of the multicoloured panels has been reconstructed from the fragments: it shows a central slab of blue-green and green veined marble as though a single sheet had been split through the middle and opened out, the two halves being placed side by side. This centrepiece was surrounded by a highly complex frame composed of painted mouldings and fillets of varying coloured marbles. A simple verbal description makes the decor sound tasteless and oppressive but it must be remembered

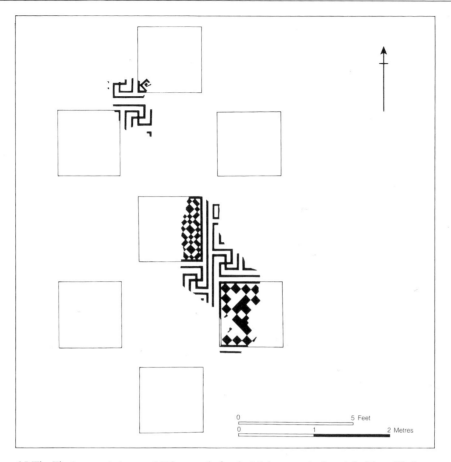

35 The Flavian mosaic in room N13 exposed after the Medusa mosaic above it had been lifted

that these elaborately painted walls belonged to very large rooms (room N9 was 20ft by 29ft) floored with plain black and white mosaics. In these circumstances carefully controlled marble style painting with a correct balance between the multicoloured and plain panels could well have been visually very exciting, though perhaps more in tune with Victorian sensibilities than with those of today.

While most of the rooms were painted to represent marble inlay one at least, room N7, was inlaid with real marble in a large panel or series of panels which remained in position until the palace was finally destroyed 200 years later, when the slabs peeled off the wall and fell in heaps onto the floor (**Col 11**). A wide range of marble was employed including the local British Purbeck marble (a blue highly fossiliferous limestone) and a grey silt stone probably also from the Isle of Purbeck. The imported marbles include white crystalline marble from Turkey, a green and white veined marble from the Pyrenees, a yellow and white marble from the Haute Garonne and at least two types from Greece including one from the island of Skyros. The interior designers of the palace clearly had a wide range of the most exotic veneers available to them — no expense was spared. Although the panel had fallen from the wall it was possible to see that some of the pieces still lay in the positions relative to each other that they had occupied in situ, for example a triangle of green veined Pyrenean marble was bordered by two fillets of white Turkish marble which in turn were enclosed by strips of grey-brown silt stone, arranged so as to give the maximum contrast between the high quality shiny marble and the drabber local material. All kinds of shapes were found in such confusion that reconstruction was impossible, but it looks as though the design included arrangements of squares set diagonally within squares as well as octagons, or pentagons, placed within circles. Arrangements of this kind are well known on the continent, particularly at Herculaneum.

Room N10 also provided evidence for the use of marble mouldings carved from white Turkish marble and blue Purbeck marble, several of which lay scattered in the rubble on its floor. Others were recovered from elsewhere in the building. The Purbeck mouldings tended to be heavier than those carved from the Turkish marble, suggesting that they served as the vertical members framing doorways or recesses, while the lighter Turkish mouldings were used as horizontal cornices across the top. This view is supported by an examination of the methods of attachment of the two types; the Purbeck mouldings were simply mortared in position, which would be an acceptable method for verticals, whilst the Turkish mouldings showed signs of being clamped to the wall with small iron hooks, a type of firmer attachment which would have been essential if they were displayed in a horizontal position. In addition to framing mouldings, marble slabs carved in a variety of other ways have been found, several of the pieces belonging to large moulded panels while one unique piece of Purbeck marble was carved on its upper surface with somewhat stylized leaves. Apart from saying that it was evidently part of a large and important panel there is no indication of its form or original position.

The two rooms on the south side of the concourse both retained substantial areas of their original mosaic floors. In room N13 several areas of the black and white Flavian mosaic could be seen through a hole in the later floor which sealed it and more was uncovered in 1989 when the later mosaic was lifted for conservation. The overall design incorporated square panels containing repetitive geometric patterns set within a complex Greek key pattern (**35; Col 22**). The floor next door in room N12 is much better preserved because the room was at no subsequent period refloored; instead it was divided by a timber partition and the original mosaic allowed to serve for 200 years as the floor of both rooms (**36–9**). The pattern is an interesting combination of motifs and arrangements which recur on first-century floors on the continent: it is simply a series of cross motifs, variously patterned, arranged between square panels some containing squares-diagonally-within-squares, others stylized compass drawn rosettes, and others fleurs-de-lis. The crosses and boxes are linked together with a square and diamond background. Both ends of the floor are provided with strips of simpler patterns to help the design fit into the shape of the room. The arrangement is by no means as dull as the verbal description suggests; all the elements are carefully contrived to give the maximum visual effect — an impression of perspective, but an incomplete perspective so that the eye is confused: at one time a square might appear to stand out as a cube — but never completely, it is pulled back into reverse by some other part of the design so that the whole floor appears to move and flicker. The care with which the floor was later patched, even if skill was limited, and the fact that it was retained for so long in the divided room suggests that it remained a popular feature for some time.

36 The Flavian mosaic in room N12. Reconstruction of the original design. The broken line marks the limit of a later patch

The walls of room N12 had been elaborately painted in the Flavian period and had been allowed to remain untouched even after the partition was inserted. The dado, parts of which could be reconstructed to a height of 22in, was pink splashed with deep red to look rather like an expensive granite and above this would have been panels painted to resemble even more exotic stones: deep red splashed with black and white, yellow painted with sinuous red veins, speckled deep blue and green and areas of greyish-white

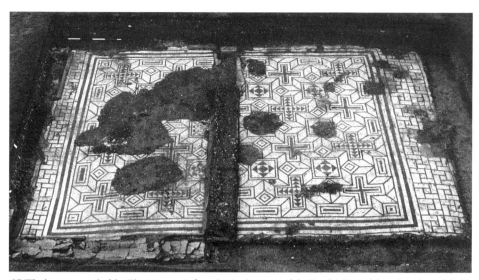

37 *The best preserved of the Flavian mosaic floors lay in the centre of the North Wing of the palace (room N12). Its black and white design gives the impression of incomplete perspective. During the third period the room was divided by a timber partition which had been plastered and painted. Later the room was used for storage. Painted plaster from one of the wall faces has fallen back into the robber trench for the wall (bottom left)*

with red veins. Like the arrangement in room N9 these richly textured areas were enclosed by strips and fillets of other 'marbles' to make up highly ornate panels relieved with intervening areas of plain red and deep blue. While the basic arrangements in rooms N9 and 12 were very close, the marbling was different. The painters must have had an enormous repertoire as well as a desire that no two rooms should look the same. Yet another composition was adopted in room N13 where the dado was of orange-red splashed with green with areas of plain red and finely painted marbling above.

Nowhere at Fishbourne is there any firm evidence of furniture or fittings, nor should any be expected to survive the 200 years of use and subsequent destruction, but some hints of the positions of furniture may be given by the arrangements of the mosaics. Those with overall patterns would not be spoilt by thoughtless placing, but in the case of room W6 with its 'mat and carpet' it is clear that certain areas were meant to be looked at. In room N13 a patch of burning on the original mosaic hints at the use of braziers to provide warmth during long winter evenings. The architect, presumably unused to designing for the British climate, had omitted to provide central heating. Braziers were a commonly used but less satisfactory alternative. Room N12 also shows signs of discoloration by fire but unlike room N13, where the early mosaic was sealed by a later floor, the mosaic in room N12 was in use at the time of the final conflagration. In this case burning rafters are a more likely cause.

East of the central suite lay a second colonnaded garden overlooked by a large room, N16, the equivalent of N7 to the west. This part of the building had suffered considerably from subsidence and from deliberate dismantling long before the final destruction and in consequence, very little other than foundations survives. Part of one of the columns from the courtyard lay in the general rubble and from the garden area came a small fragment of painted wall plaster depicting a fluted urn from a garden scene,

38, 39 Details of motifs incorporated into the mosaic in room N12.

presumably once painted on the wall backing the colonnade. It is an interesting reminder that not all the walls simulated marble inlay. As we shall see later some of the freer painting is of extremely high quality.

The eastern suite of the North Wing, rooms N18–23, contained some of the finest mosaics to survive in the palace. The general arrangement of the rooms differs from the other two North Wing suites in that there is no obvious concourse, but the plan would demand that room N19 served as a general way through to rooms N10, 22 and 23 beyond, and it could well have been linked with rooms N18 and 20. The room itself was floored with a basically white mosaic simply picked out with a black geometric design. Immediately next door in room N20 was an altogether more impressive mosaic, one of the very few truly polychrome floors to be found in the palace, consisting of a central circular design set within a square (**40–1; Col 5**). The circle was composed of a twisted rope-like guilloche in a wide range of colours on a black background within which came a circular band of rosettes alternating with heart-shaped leaves both drawn in red, yellow and white, outlined in black and shown against a white background. The central circular area which lay within has unfortunately been totally destroyed, but in such a position one might have expected a finely figured centrepiece. Some idea of the quality of the mosaicist's figure drawing comes out in the designs which he fitted into the spandrels between the circular framing panels and the border of the square. Each corner was different, one had two dolphins facing a vase, another was similar but with fish instead of dolphins, whilst the remaining two contained urns with high square-topped handles and tendrils growing from their bases. All four were very skilfully drawn and carefully designed to fit the difficult triangular spaces available.

Mosaics of this kind, unknown elsewhere in Britain, are rare even in Italy but the basic arrangement of a large circular panel set within a square recurs on several of the Italian sites. What is a little less usual is the use of the complicated guilloche to enclose the centre circle. Its layout and successful execution required considerable skill and experience.

Room N21 probably served as an anteroom to N20. With its simple mosaic of black overlaid by large squares of red and blue enlivened by interlocking white frames, it would have made a striking contrast to the more delicate floral floor next door (Col 7). It is difficult to believe that the juxtaposition of these two was not deliberately contrived to make a dramatic visual impact on an unsuspecting visitor. One interesting detail survives on the border of the floor where a small diamond shape made from white tesserae is set into the black surround. Since it is so evidently not part of the design it may have been the signature of the mosaicist.

The floors of the remaining three rooms do not survive to any extent except for small patches of a simple black and white mosaic in room N22. Roman destruction and recent ploughing have removed everything else. It is a great pity that some trace of the wall decoration in rooms N20 and 21 has not survived. It would have been interesting to have seen how the designers tackled the problem posed by small rooms with multicoloured floors, for they could hardly have used the heavy style of marbling commonly employed elsewhere in rooms with simple black and white floors. A second, totally different, style is, however, known from a mass of painted wall plaster, which at some stage had been carried out of the North Wing and dumped in a hollow immediately to the west. It may have been removed when redecorating was being

The North Wing

40, 41 The finest of the surviving coloured mosaics in the Flavian palace lay in room N20 of the North Wing. The central circular panel is now missing, but around it was a band of alternating rosettes and vine leaves enclosed by a twisted guilloche. The corners were filled by different motifs incorporating central vases with tendrils or fish on either side. A wide range of colours was used

carried out early in the second century, or alternatively when the east end of the wing was demolished a little later. At any event its original position cannot now be recovered. The quality of the work is extremely fine. Basically the walls were painted yellow and upon this even background two types of isolated panels were drawn, one in various tones of plain untextured red representing recesses, the edges carefully shaded and the corners mitred to give the impression of depth; the others were scenes which might have appeared as distant views seen through windows. Between the recesses and scenes the yellow walls were enlivened with simple foliage in green and brown with exquisitely painted rose-buds.

One fragment showing the corner of a scene is of particular significance (Col 10). The picture, painted with a restricted colour range of blue, brown and white, shows part of the front elevation of a colonnaded building with the sea in the background. It is brilliantly executed with simple brush strokes recapturing the quality of a choppy sea and sunlit building, but what is even more important is that an almost identical painting is known at Stabiae, one of the towns to suffer during the eruption of Vesuvius in AD 79. The same colour range, similar subject matter (a harbour scene at Stabiae) and an identical, almost impressionistic, style of brushwork strongly suggests that the two paintings were carried out by the same school of artists if not by the same man. This one small fragment is perhaps the most dramatic link of all between Flavian Fishbourne and the contemporary metropolitan world.

The superstructure of the North Wing is relatively easy to reconstruct in outline. The verandas of the gardens would have had inward-sloping roofs above which the walls of the rooms would have risen so that clear-storey light could have been provided. In all probability the three main blocks were roofed with north–south pitched roofs ending on three imposing gables overlooking the great garden. East–west roofs of lower pitch would have been sufficient to cover the rest. The only means of access needed would have been two doors opening from the southern fronting colonnade into the peristyles of the two private gardens. Such an arrangement would have afforded the maximum amount of peace for the residents.

It will be seen from the above description that the North Wing was planned and built on a grand scale with private colonnaded gardens, suites of spacious rooms and elaborate interior decoration. There can be little doubt that it was designed as a residential wing to provide luxurious accommodation — possibly for visitors. The plan would have allowed it to have been used as at least three separate suites.

The South Wing

The discovery and reconstruction of the South Wing was in many ways one of the most satisfying parts of the entire excavation, partly because it was unexpected but largely because with a minimum expenditure of energy one of the major problems of the site was suddenly and conclusively solved. We realised that the south side of the great courtyard, defined by the East, North and West Wings, was closed in some way either by a range of rooms, a plain wall or, more likely we thought, by a simple colonnaded walk to allow a view from the garden courtyard south to the sea. But it was not until the summer of 1967, the last major season, that the owners of a house on the south side of the main road invited us to excavate in their garden to address the question. One of the first trenches cut in the courtyard behind the house revealed the footings for a stylobate, which once supported a colonnade, and the trench where the ground-level gutter had lain immediately in front of it. The discovery was not particularly spectacular but in terms of the ground plan it was of vital importance, for it showed not only that a major range of rooms existed across the south but that it was provided with a south-facing view worthy of a colonnade. A few further trial trenches dug in the front garden confirmed the existence of the range and allowed two of the cross walls to be planned. In the following year details of the east end of the wing were examined in the front garden of another house.

These small fragments of ground plan, in conjunction with what is known of the rest of the palace, allowed the general shape of the wing to be reconstructed, since the south side is known and the north side can be fixed, supposing that it was symmetrically sited in relation to the central east–west axis which passed through the audience chamber. Similarly the east end has been defined by excavation, while the west probably lay in the same relationship to the West Wing, as does the end of the North Wing. Based on these calculations the range of rooms would be some 52ft wide by 272ft long with colonnades on both the north and south sides — a remarkable return in information for the effort expended on so few trial trenches.

One interesting problem to be raised is how much of the Flavian South Wing incorporated rooms of the Neronian proto-palace and how much was built onto it in the Flavian period. The structures examined in the centre of the wing are constructed in the style of the Flavian work, but those at the extreme east end are clearly part of the earlier building which had simply been absorbed into the new palace. The junction lies somewhere between and is not yet available for study.

Little can be said of the interior decoration of this South Wing largely because of the intensive robbing to which the area has been subjected, as well as the destructive effects of road building and the construction of the present houses, but it must have been in this area that the black and white mosaic pavement was found when the road was widened in 1805. The excavations have also produced loose *tesserae* and pieces of painted wall plaster, leaving little doubt that the wing was finely adorned.

The nature of the superstructure depends upon the internal arrangement of the rooms which at present is ill-known. The simplest reconstruction would be to suppose that the range was roofed beneath a single continuous roof with gables at each end, but such an arrangement while functionally adequate would have been visually so dull that the monotony must have been relieved with cross ridges and other elaborations to break up the single sweep.

That the wing faced south across a private garden, which we will see was elaborately landscaped, strongly suggests that it was a residential range of some significance, quite possibly the private residence of the owner. If this is accepted it will explain one difficulty which had hitherto remained — the siting of the bath suite in the extreme south-east corner of the palace. All the time that the North Wing was thought to be the owner's residence it was puzzling why the bath suite should be so far away — nearly five minutes walk on a wet night. The discovery of the South Wing and its tentative identification as the owner's suite neatly overcomes the problem, for the baths were now conveniently close, at the end of the corridor.

The East Wing

The East Wing, nearly 500ft long, was an amalgam of several different architectural features strung out and given visual unity by a colonnade facing into the garden and an impressive monumental east front — the face which the palace presented to the outside world. In the centre lay the entrance hall, the visual and functional axis of the wing, while in the far north-east corner was a great aisled hall also provided with an imposing façade. Between them lay two colonnaded gardens flanked by a single range of rooms. The arrangement south of the entrance hall is altogether more confused, partly by the superincumbent modern buildings and partly because of the integration of the earlier proto-palace into the new design. The general impression gained is that a certain symmetry was arrived at by regarding the peristyle of the proto-palace, and a rather awkward wedge-shaped space created between it and the entrance hall, as equivalent to the two courtyards on the north side and incorporating the rooms of the proto-palace into a range again reflecting a similar arrangement to the north. To complete the balance a monumental façade would have been needed to front the bath suite, but the area has not been extensively examined and no positive evidence for this has yet come to light.

It was the entrance hall that was meant to impress the most, for through here all visitors had to pass (**42**). Hardly surprising, therefore, that it was designed as the largest room in the entire palace, 80ft wide by 105ft long. It was provided at its east and west fronts with enormous pedimented façades, each supported on six large columns standing to a height of about 26ft. Internally the room consisted of the main hall with a series of small rooms or cubicles opening out of each side. This arrangement was partly structural, so as to provide additional lateral support across the enormous distance which would otherwise have had to be roofed, and partly for visual effect, to create interesting spaces only incompletely seen from any one position so that a visitor would have been encouraged to move on to examine them. Incomplete vistas of this kind were frequently employed by Roman architects, particularly when there was a need to create a flow of people to prevent congestion. In terms of the superstructure at Fishbourne it is probable that the 'cubicles' were spaced behind continuous side arcades, the arcade walls thus reducing the greatest span of the area to 49ft, which was quite manageable as far as availability of timber for ceiling and rafters was concerned. As the reconstruction suggests, the alcoves were probably provided with lower ceilings than the main hall, but high enough to allow large lunettes to be placed in the side walls. Lunettes in this position would have been essential to allow light into the hall and the brightly lit alcoves themselves opening from behind arcades would have provided attractive settings for statuary.

Two footings were discovered running across the hall, dividing off bays at each end. The western footing was sufficiently well preserved to show that for most of its length it was a 'sleeper wall', i.e. a below floor-level footing, which supported two rectangular pier bases evenly placed on either side of the central axis. These bases show beyond doubt that the hall was divided at this point by a screen wall composed of a large central arch flanked by two narrower, and therefore correspondingly lower, side arches. The equivalent footing at the east end was too badly robbed for any trace of superstructure to survive but here, too, one may suppose there to have been a similar arrangement. The general effect of these internal divisions would have been to isolate the central part of the hall from the outside world, to give it a feeling of unity and to prevent it from becoming a characterless tunnel leading through the wing.

One final refinement may be mentioned: in the western bay a small pool was built surrounded by a raised step and probably originally lined with sheets of marble. It was possible to trace the position of the water inlet, the size of the trench in which it was set suggesting a pipe of lead, leading to the centre of the pool where some form of fountain mechanism would have been adopted. The outfall, once composed of standard ceramic water-pipes, was found leading to the ground-level gutter surrounding the garden. A fountain in this position would have been visually very pleasing, particularly when viewed through the screen wall from the main hall. It would have focused attention on the view beyond while at the same time emphasizing the scale of the hall itself.

Apart from the structural consideration laid out above, we know very little of the interior decoration of the hall, largely because it was allowed to become ruinous during the Roman period and little now survives. Its floors, however, were of mortar while some at least of the walls were painted in panels of red. A marble cornice moulding was also recovered from the rubble. The general impression given by the surviving remains is that the finish was not particularly exceptional. All the skill of the architect was centred upon the form of the superstructure, its contrived vistas, its volumes and its feelings of lightness. Carefully controlled proportions at the expense of decorative detail is a perfectly acceptable order of priorities in an entrance hall of this kind. A modern equivalent might be the entrance hall of a large railway station in which functional considerations are uppermost. The analogy might be somewhat misleading, for there can be little doubt that the Fishbourne entrance hall was a brilliantly conceived structure, far superior to most of the contemporary Roman buildings in the country.

The second large structural element in the East Wing was the aisled hall built at the north-east corner of the palace in the angle between the East and North Wings, facing east (**43**). It was simpler in structure than the entrance hall, consisting of a single room 70ft by 90ft divided into a 'nave' and two side aisles by four pairs of massively constructed piers which would originally have supported two parallel arcades (**44**). All that now survives of the superstructure are two of the pier bases, single blocks of limestone 3ft square and 12in thick. An examination of the foundations for the bases shows that they were all designed to support considerable weight, probably taking most of the vertical thrust from the roof, while the lateral thrust would have been absorbed by the side walls. Allowing for the roof tiles, the timber rafters and the rafter nails, a conservative estimate for the weight of the roof would be about 125 tons.

The structural details of the aisled hall would probably have been very much like those employed in the entrance hall with the central nave enclosed by a high ceiling, the aisles with somewhat lower ones but still high enough to allow large windows to be placed high up in the side walls, high because they would have had to be well above the adjacent roof lines, as the reconstruction drawing suggests, so as not to be obscured. The only entrance would have been in the centre of the east side, in front of which a massive pedimented front supported on six columns would almost certainly have been constructed to form an impressive façade to the building behind, and at the same time to balance with the façade of the entrance hall.

The building of the Flavian Palace

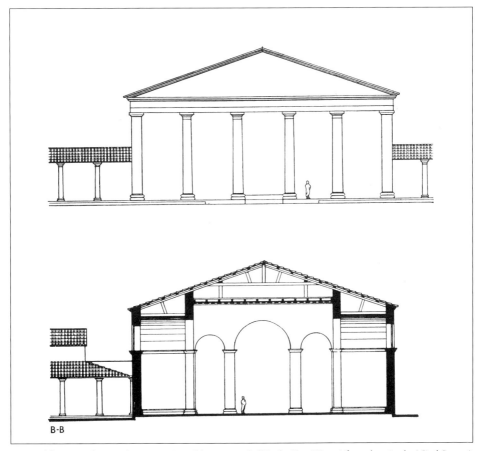

42 (and facing) Architectural reconstruction of the entrance hall in the East Wing (after a drawing by Nigel Sunter)

The function of the building is not altogether clear, but its comparative isolation from the rest of the palace and the fact that it opens to the outside world suggests a semi-public use, and one strong possibility is that it served as an assembly hall similar to those found in Domitian's palace. A place of assembly for the dependents of the estate and for the owner's clients would have been essential in a palace of this size. The siting of the aisled hall and its simple functional plan would have suited it admirably for this use.

An interesting series of alterations were made to the hall at an early stage in its life. Masonry pedestals were attached to the inner faces of the first three pairs of piers, and on the central axis of the far end a large masonry base was provided. These cannot have had anything to do with increasing the load-bearing capacity of the piers because their footings were too insubstantial, and indeed several of them showed some signs of subsidence. In fact, the general positioning leaves little doubt that they were in some way connected with visual embellishments, quite possibly supporting statues or, in the case of the central base, a group of statuary. This would have been quite in keeping with a place of public assembly. Indeed it is possible that the hall had religious overtones — a place where people might be expected to offer up public sacrifices for the well-being of the emperor's household. The implications are extremely interesting but sadly

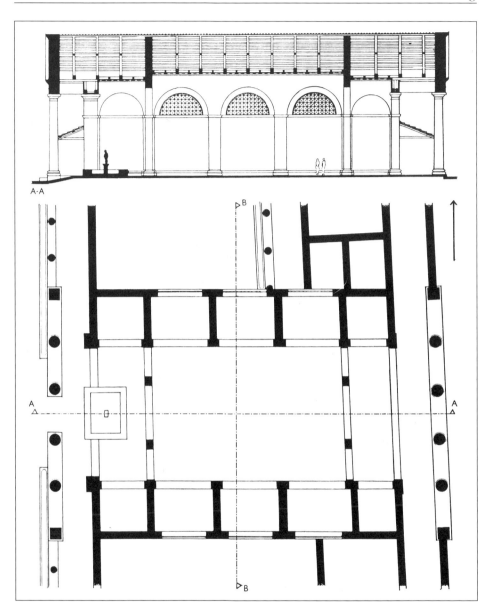

beyond the scope of the archaeological evidence.

Between the aisled hall and entrance hall were two courtyards flanked by a range of eleven rooms. The northern courtyard, the larger of the two, was surrounded on three sides by a colonnaded veranda facing inwards towards a garden and closed on the fourth side by a blank wall (**60–1**). The southern courtyard was provided with colonnades along only two of its sides. Together the two gardens would have formed quiet open spaces for walking and relaxation for the use of those residing in the range of rooms to the east.

The rooms themselves had all suffered very considerably from late Roman and post-

The building of the Flavian Palace

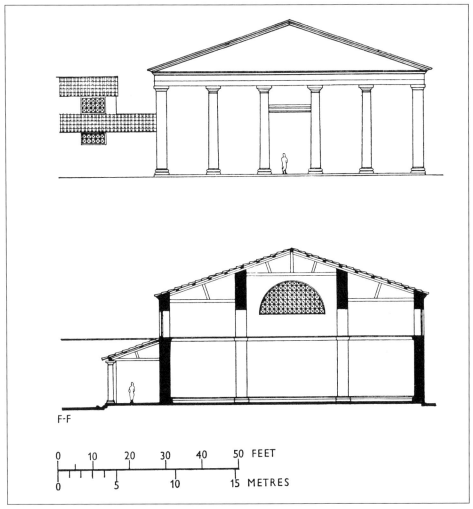

43 (and facing) Architectural reconstruction of the aisled hall in the north-east corner of the palace (after a drawing by Nigel Sunter)

Roman destruction and robbing, and apart from loose tesserae in room E6 and a few fragments of painted plaster in the style of that commonly found in the North Wing nothing of the interior decoration remains. The ground plan, however, is instructive. The rooms seem to have been deliberately built in suites consisting of one large and two smaller rooms, such as the groups made by E1–3, E4–6 and E9–11. Rooms E7 and 8 may possibly belong to a fourth set. Very similar arrangements are to be found in the official hotels (*mansiones*), particularly those at Richborough and Silchester. It is probable that here, too, we are dealing with rooms for official travellers of low rank who could not expect to be offered the sumptuous guest suites in the North Wing. The East Wing suites were nevertheless comfortable and were, after all, provided with gardens even if they had to be shared with neighbours. Their only real disadvantage would have been the noise made by people using the entrance hall, the side street and the aisled hall.

The East Wing

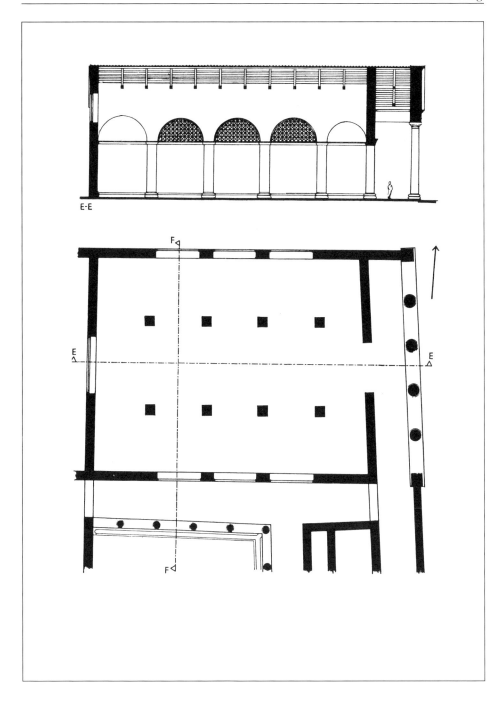

The building of the Flavian Palace

44 The aisled hall lay in the corner between the North and East Wings. The main weight of its 70ft span roof was taken on eight piers, the bases for which were massively constructed. The foundation of each was of flint set in concrete supporting a base of ashlar masonry and tiles. On this was placed a single large foundation block. The original floor would have been level with the base of the block. Towards the end of the first century additional bases were added, possibly to support statuary

The superstructure of this area is simple to reconstruct. The rooms would probably have been covered by a single pitched roof ending on gables before the walls of the two halls were reached.

The garden peristyles had the usual inward sloping type of roof supported on columns around the edge of the garden, and attached to the wall of the main range low enough to allow for windows into the rooms. Along the east side of the range ran a corridor leading between the porches of the entrance hall and aisled hall. It is difficult to be sure of its architectural treatment but there is some evidence to suggest that it was not colonnaded but was divided from the street by a plain blank wall provided with sufficient windows to allow in the necessary light. Such an arrangement would have given some privacy to the occupants of the range and cut down the volume of noise penetrating from outside.

South of the entrance hall the arrangement of the rooms and courtyards reflected as far as possible the plan on the north side. The peristyle of the proto-palace was retained largely intact to be an equivalent of the larger of the courtyards on the north, while a smaller courtyard seems to have been created between it and the hall to balance the smaller one on the other side of the hall. The range of rooms belonging to the old proto-palace was also retained and was continued up to the south side of the hall by a small block of new rooms.

How the baths themselves fared is difficult to say. There seem to have been comparatively few alterations except the extension of the room which contained the original *tepidarium*, but it must be admitted that several incompletely examined structures extend from the south side of the suite and that these may well belong to Flavian modifications.

The main structural elements of the Flavian palace have now been summarized so far as the present evidence allows, but the building and its interior decoration is only one part of the complex. As we will see in the chapter to follow, they were set in a carefully constructed environment created with the same vision and skill as that lavished on the upstanding structures. Only when the surroundings have been described can we begin to appreciate the full significance of the whole conception.

7. The gardens and the environment

In 1964 a trial trench was cut from the East Wing into the large central area enclosed by the four wings, specifically to examine the soil within the potential garden area. Much to our surprise, in addition to finding the original Roman topsoil, three slots were discovered running parallel to the building. They were filled with a green loamy soil which had been marled with lime to counteract the slight acidity hereabouts. That they were bedding trenches for plants seemed possible but first it was necessary to see more of them in plan. In the following year, 1965, two areas were chosen for further exploration, one in the northern part of the courtyard and the other close to the north side of the entrance hall where, if the slots were bedding trenches, they might be expected to stop to allow access across the garden. The results were convincing, for not only were water-pipes and posts of fences uncovered in the northern half, but the bedding trenches by the entrance hall were found to turn to form part of a façade apparently running across the garden and defining the north side of the path. That there was a formal garden discoverable by excavation was clear: the next question to be asked 'What is the form of the garden?' took two years of consolidated effort to answer.

Before considering the garden plan it is necessary to say something of the problems facing those who first laid it out and to describe the setting for their creation. We have already seen how at the time of the construction hundreds of tons of gravel and clay were shifted to create a level platform for the North, East and South Wings and the garden between them. This levelling must first have been preceded by the stripping of the topsoil and its stockpiling somewhere for reuse when the levelling was complete. Then clay and gravel were removed from the western part of the site and tipped over the low-lying eastern area to form the almost level platform, 250ft by 320ft, of barren, ill-drained clay hardly conducive to luxurious growth. But by spreading the marled topsoil back over the clay and by digging deep bedding trenches wherever shrubs were to be planted, a hospitable environment was created in which the newly planted garden could begin to flourish.

The garden was completely surrounded by colonnaded walks, on the north, east and south, laid out at ground level and on the west side supported on the 5ft high revetting wall. The colonnades were continuous and of a uniform height except at the centre of the west side, where steps led up to the porch of the audience chamber, and in the centre of the East Wing in front of the entrance hall, which was here provided with a

The gardens and the environment

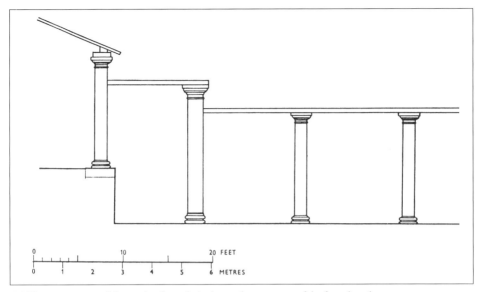

45 The arrangement of the north colonnade in the north-east corner of the formal garden

monumental hexastyle façade. The general spacing of the columns of the colonnades is given by three which remain in position on the stylobate in the north-west corner of the garden, 11ft apart (**45–7; Col 17–18**). Elsewhere extensive robbing has removed not only the columns themselves but also the stylobate blocks and the ground-level stone gutters in front. Knowing the spacing, however, and having sufficient pieces of their capitals and bases, it is possible to estimate that originally the columns were about 12ft high, with the tiled roof of the veranda sloping up to the walls behind. The verandas were therefore high and wide.

The faces of the inner walls were plastered and painted. From the large quantity of fragments found in the north-west corner it is possible to show that, while still influenced by the concept of marble panelling, the decorators adopted a simplified and lighter style with a white dado splashed red and ochre surmounted by a plain white wall divided into panels with wide red bands, the panels being enlivened with simple diamond-shaped inner frames painted in red or green. The entire scheme must have been carefully chosen to suit the great expanse of wall presented by the verandas; it was sufficiently interesting to break the monotony but at the same time simple enough not to conflict with the sharp vertical emphasis of the colonnades. Like the painting elsewhere in the palace it shows a fine regard for the overall visual context.

A certain structural problem was provided at the north-west (and presumably the south-west) corners of the garden where the low-level colonnades of the North and South Wings abutted the higher level of the West Wing, but this was neatly overcome by providing a flight of timber steps between the two levels and raising the height of the lower colonnade in two steps by making the westernmost column about $2\frac{1}{2}$ft higher, and of correspondingly larger diameter, and using it to support an architrave on different levels (**45**). In this way sufficient head-room was provided. With a certain embellishment of the roof line at this point, perhaps with elaborate finials, the functional solution could have been turned to a positive visual advantage in enlivening

The gardens and the environment

46 The north-west corner of the formal garden of the Flavian palace. The modern building (background) is constructed exactly upon the walls of the Roman North Wing. In front is a veranda and stylobate with three column bases still in position. At the west (left-hand) side the stylobate abuts the revetting wall in front of the West Wing. The ground-level gutter is well preserved in this section. The narrow trenches, some of them now water-filled, are the bedding trenches for shrubs or bushes flanking the pathways. A length of ceramic water-pipe can be seen along the west side of the west path

the western façade and offering counterpoised points of interest balanced about the central audience chamber.

The presence of the veranda roofs sloping inwards towards the garden meant that great volumes of rain-water would have poured into the garden gutter which lay at ground level in front of the stylobate, a gutter composed of massive limestone and greensand slabs with a deeply hollowed upper surface. The garden was drained in two halves, the northern half towards the north-east corner and the southern half to one of the southern corners. The arrangement at the north-east corner shows that from here the water was led into a tile-built culvert, which passed beneath the veranda, and reappeared in the northern East Wing courtyard, running along the open gutter for a distance before disappearing again beneath the floor levels and the street in a culvert, which eventually opened into the canalized stream flanking the east side of the palace complex. The course of the southern outfall may have been equally tortuous but the crucial area has not been excavated. The system is even more impressive when it is known that both of the North Wing courtyards as well as a small court on the north side of the entrance hall poured their contents out into the garden gutter through tile-built culverts laid beneath the verandas. Since the run-off from the adjacent roofs would also have found its way over the verandas and into the various courtyard gutters, it can be

The gardens and the environment

47 The north-west corner of the main formal garden of the palace, showing the stylobate and gutter fronting the veranda with fragments of the columns lying where they had fallen. In the corner is the masonry foundation for a water tank

The gardens and the environment

48 One of the column capitals found in the East Wing of the palace; columns of this type, 11-12 ft high, would have stood at 11ft intervals around the gardens of the palace. Some of the stone from which they were made came from Gloucestershire, some from France

seen that at least half of the rain falling on the northern half of the palace was drained from the building by the single culvert in the north-east corner. The levelling of the drains was meticulously accurate: along the west front from the audience chamber steps to the north-west corner the fall was 0.77ft (1 in 183) and from here to the north-east corner it was 1.80ft (1 in 139). The capacity of the culvert also increased, that in the north-east corner having a cross section of 150 sq in. Even so it is difficult to believe that the system always functioned efficiently, particularly in torrential downpours.

So much then for the masonry backdrop to the garden, but what of the garden itself? The basic plan to which the gardeners worked was simple. A central path 40 ft wide was laid out across the garden from east to west, linking the entrance hall and audience chamber with the equivalent of a processional way, while subsidiary side paths were constructed to skirt the garden in front of the colonnades. All the paths were defined by bedding trenches (**46–7, 49–51**).

The bedding trenches flanking the central path were arranged in a regular ornate fashion to create a series of large semicircular and rectangular recesses alternating with each other (**49, 51; Col 14–15**). Apart from the first and last recesses of the row, each was defined by two parallel bedding trenches, while the length of straight façade between them was composed of three trenches. If we are correct in assuming that the trenches supported continuous hedges of a shrub, like box, then either the multiple

49 One of the bedding trenches flanking the central path in the formal garden of the Flavian palace. The trench was cut through gravel and was filled with loam. The recess contains a single bedding pit presumably for a large bush or tree

rows were allowed to grow together into one solid mass, or, more likely, they were kept clipped as individual hedges. The centres of the recesses were carefully examined to see if trees or shrubs had been planted in them, but apart from the easternmost semicircular alcoves, where bedding pits indicate some form of growth, the others were without floral embellishment. Originally, however, they may well have been deliberately constructed to display groups of statuary, urns or other pieces of garden furniture.

While the entire northern façade has been excavated, most of the southern side of the path lies beneath the gardens of modern houses where it is largely inaccessible. However, the first (easternmost) recess on the southern side lay within the excavation area and has proved to be almost an exact reflection of the northern side. Moreover, where, in one of the modern gardens, it was possible to check the western end of the façade again a close correspondence with the north side can be demonstrated. It seems reasonable therefore to assume that the two sides of the centre path were symmetrical.

A great expanse of hedge-lined pathway running from one side of the garden to the other would have looked impressive enough, particularly with groups of statuary in the alcoves, but there were additional elaborations to give scale to the concept. On the central axis in front of the steps leading up to the audience chamber was a square foundation made of tiles set in pink mortar, presumably part of a statue base. A single figure standing here on a raised plinth would have looked magnificent against the columns of the audience chamber. In an equivalent position at the east end of the path a substantial soil-filled pit was found, but there is no evidence of its date or function. Its regular spacing in relation to the main east–west axis would imply that it was constructed as part of the garden layout but what manner of superstructure it took is beyond recovery.

The gardens and the environment

50 The north-east corner of the formal garden, looking south. In the foreground is the robber trench for the gutter which once flanked the northern colonnade. The bedding trenches can be clearly seen, delineating the edges of the paths. Two lengths of water-pipe are visible: the curved stretch originally ran unhindered from the water-tower in the north-west corner of the garden to the area south of the central path; the straighter length served fountains arranged around the northern paths

From the west end of the central path, side paths ran along the front of the West Wing; the one on the north has been completely excavated. It was about 12ft wide and lined on both sides with hedges represented now by bedding trenches of the same kind as those delineating the central path. On the east side, against the central area of the garden, two trenches had been dug, the one nearest the path kinking in at regular intervals towards a straight one behind. The trenches on the west side, towards the building, were more complex in layout, consisting of two parallel straight lines with a third, close to the edge of the path, returning at regular intervals to meet the middle trench, creating small recesses equivalent to those on the opposite side. One particularly interesting feature of these western trenches is that the rows were of differing depths, the deepest being against the wall. It is tempting here to remember the description which Pliny gives of his Tuscan garden, in which he says that one of the garden walls was hidden behind banks of hedges which gradually increased in height.

The revetting wall for the West Wing was regarded as a structural feature to be hidden. This was done by plastering the wall, painting it a uniform deep green background colour, and over this painting a range of vegetation including great leafy fronds and stems with tendrils growing up them. Behind these an on-looker was allowed to glimpse a garden scene beyond with its garden features of lattice-work picked out in white. In fact the West Wing wall was camouflaged to give the impression of yet another garden.

The western bedding trenches, in front of the revetting wall, ended with a large pit which had been deliberately dug into the clay and filled with garden soil. A close examination of the sides of the pit suggested the possibility that roots had penetrated out into the clay implying the presence of a substantial growth, probably a tree. Visually a tree here would have been hugely acceptable, partly to obscure the slight incongruity in the different levels of the colonnade roof and partly to hide a water tank. It would also have added an attractive emphasis to the end of the West Wing colonnade and would presumably have been balanced by another at the south-west corner.

The path along the north side of the garden was very much like the west path except that the recesses in the garden-side hedge were omitted (**Col 16**). The east path was, however, altogether different, for while a façade of bedding trenches was maintained in front of the colonnade there were no bedding trenches along the garden side of the path except for shallow discontinuous slots which could have resulted from the planting of small herbaceous flowers. In fact the central area of the garden was open to the east path, unlike the other three sides where hedges intervened.

While the north half of the garden has been almost totally excavated, very little work has been possible in the southern half except at the eastern side where limited trial trenching has shown that the bedding trenches along the east colonnade reflect those to the north of the central path.

The garden, then, was divided by means of hedge-lined paths into two halves which could have been laid out either with a wilderness of vegetation, like that shown on the famous wall painting in the Garden Room of Livia at the Prima Porta, or it could have been kept as short-mown grass. On balance the evidence would seem to point to grass, partly because luxuriant vegetation would have obscured the carefully contrived views and partly because, in spite of extensive and careful excavation of most of the central area, only one solitary bedding pit was discovered: it is most unlikely therefore that deep-rooted plants could have grown in the area.

The one bedding pit is very carefully sited so that the tree which it supported would have appeared towards the centre of the line of vision of a person standing in the centre of the West Wing and looking towards the North Wing (51; Col 15). Anyone who stands here today can appreciate the value of the tree which has been replanted on this spot, in relieving the monotony of the front of the North Wing — the strong vertical emphasis of a mature tree is exactly what is needed to counteract the horizontality of the wing. This point raises an even more important one: how was the front of the East Wing enlivened when viewed from the west? Structurally the centre was provided with the pedimented front of the entrance hall but on each side was a continuous and highly repetitive colonnade stretching for 130ft; such visual boredom would have been unacceptable, but in the hands of the brilliant landscape gardener the problem was overcome with simple elegance. The bedding trench closest to the east colonnade was filled not with the marled loam used elsewhere, but with a thick black occupation rubbish of the kind which the Elder Pliny suggests was suitable for bedding roses. This fact, taken in conjunction with a number of post-holes hereabouts, which imply some form of timber structure, possibly lattice-work, strongly suggests that a type of climbing plant was grown. A further point, apparent on the plan, is that the outer bedding trench, which for part of its length turned back on the middle trench in the manner of the trenches elsewhere, was replaced by a straight trench along the south part of the path

The gardens and the environment

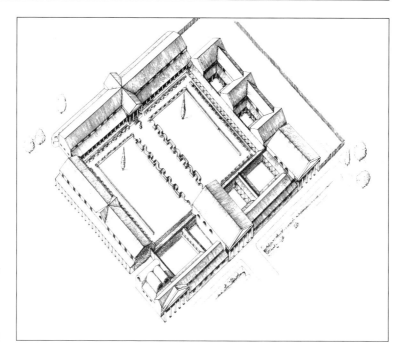

51 Reconstruction of the Flavian palace and its formal garden (by David Neal)

and was associated with post-holes. Here again the implication is of a different type of vegetation, possibly climbers arranged to become denser towards the central path. If this arrangement was repeated to the south of the central path, the break in the vegetation to provide access to the west façade of the entrance hall would have been visually dramatic.

This was not all: 35ft in front of the colonnade a second screen was created consisting of trees alternating with substantial upright timbers, represented now by bedding pits of black soil and stone-packed post-holes. There can be very little doubt that we are dealing here with evidence of some kind of flowering tree which it was necessary to train along a timber framework. The Younger Pliny writing of one of his gardens describes how in one place there was 'a row of fruit trees alternating with posts to give an air of rural simplicity in surroundings of otherwise studied formality'. Rural simplicity is hardly a term which could be used of the Fishbourne garden but this kind of arrangement was probably widely adopted in the Roman world. The function of the screen would have been to add interest to the view looking east and by returning the posts for a short distance along the north side the eastern façade was cleverly integrated with the rest of the building. This is yet another example of the landscape gardener's great skill.

Nothing has yet been said of the plants growing in the garden. It was at one stage hoped that the soil from the bedding trenches would produce identifiable pollen, but the conditions were not conducive to survival and all that remained were a few grains of the tougher pollen such as hawkweed, daisy and other weeds of cultivation. We have therefore to rely on classical sources, both literature and painting, to give some idea of what might have been grown. In Italy the favourite hedging plant, referred to constantly by Pliny, was box which is known to have grown in Britain during the Roman period. The careful marling of the soil in the bedding trenches for the Fishbourne hedges would have created suitable conditions for the shrub, but while the presence of box is likely we cannot be certain of its use here. Other plants would probably have included roses and fruit trees, as we have seen, and there may have been a host of other smaller flowers including perhaps rosemary, lily and acanthus — all popular flowers in the Roman period.

The garden was supplied with fresh water by means of an extensive, and no doubt expensive, system of ceramic pipes set beneath the paths (**46, 50**). Excavation to the east of the palace between 1985 and 1995 identified the line of an aqueduct running towards the north-east corner of the building where there may have been a collecting tank. From there water was led, by means of an aqueduct, along the north wall of the North Wing, then along the west wall, into a settling tank built in the north-west corner of the garden. Part of the aqueduct, constructed of roof tiles in clay and mortar, still survives but unfortunately it lay almost exactly in the path of the 1960 water-main trench and was largely destroyed by it. The last length of the supply, passing through the corner of the West Wing to the tank, was conducted by means of ceramic water-pipes set in a clay-lined trench to prevent leakage. The tank was built on a stone foundation which projected into the corner of the garden. Originally it would have been of timber, perhaps lined with lead, but no trace of the superstructure has survived. The function of a tank in this position was twofold: to form a reservoir with a sufficient head of water to serve the garden and to allow sediment to settle out. This last point was of particular importance because had muddy water been allowed into the pipes they would soon have become blocked, causing serious problems.

From the tank the water was fed into several ceramic pipe-lines embedded in the clay beneath the paths. Each pipe-line was composed of individual pipes 18in long and 8in in diameter with an internal bore of 4in. Their ends were so made that one socketed neatly into the other, making a firm joint which was then sealed with a hard white mortar. The first pipe-line ran along the north edge of the north path and turned at right-angles in the north-east corner to take up a similar position along the east side as far as the central path, where the main pipe stopped and a subsidiary branch led to the pool in the entrance hall. The pipe was designed to take water to a series of basins or fountains set along the path, possibly in the recesses in the hedges. The second pipe ran untapped along the centre of the north and east paths, but after crossing the central path it veered towards the hedge and from here on it presumably served the fountains lining the path. It had, in fact, taken over the function of the first pipe in the southern part of the garden. This implies that while the tank could provide a sufficient head of water to service a considerable number of fountains, its energy had been spent by the time the entrance hall was reached. The southern part of the garden had therefore to be provided with a separate supply. A third pipe ran from the tank south along the west path, apparently serving fountains along the entire length of the West Wing. How the south side of the garden was supplied, whether by the continuation of the second or third pipe or a combination of both, is unknown.

We have referred to fountains and basins arranged along the paths but it must be admitted that no structure of this kind has been found in position. This is hardly surprising for the building had a long life after the great garden had ceased to be maintained, during which time objects such as basins and their lead fittings were probably carried off for reuse. Since they would have needed no footing, little trace can be expected to remain. Fragments of several of the basins have, however, survived in rubble deposits about the palace. The most substantial of these is a semicircular basin more than 3ft in diameter carved from a solid slab of Purbeck marble. A basin of this kind would probably have been set at ground level with water gently bubbling into it. A fragment of a more elaborate basin was found discarded in a late well cut through one of the East Wing courtyards; again it was carved from Purbeck marble but it seems to have once been provided with legs slotted into the underside. No doubt a wide variety of different types were in use, as indeed contemporary wall paintings of Roman gardens suggest. When the fountains at Fishbourne were turned on there would have been no great shows of water gushing high in the air, but instead gentle streams bubbling up in the basins set around the paths, the waste water trickling away into the gutters behind the hedges.

Enough has been said of the great formal garden to give some idea of its Roman form and the way in which it was meticulously contrived to fit into, and indeed to enhance, the surrounding palace. It was essentially a show-piece, there to set off the building to the wonder of visitors and to demonstrate to second generation provincials the sophistication of Roman culture.

The formal garden enclosed within the wings of the palace was essentially a semi-public area open to all acceptable visitors, but as we have seen it was only the West Wing, itself the official range, which opened onto it. The rooms of the North Wing and of the residential parts of the East Wing were provided with their own private gardens surrounded with quiet colonnaded walks. One has only to read Pliny's description of his gardens in Italy to understand how a sensitive Roman appreciated them; wandering around he was delighted by their surprising contrasts, by the soft grass beneath his feet, by the interplay of light and shade in a wooded glade; Pliny loved nature itself, not human contrivance. It is no surprise, then, that when we turn away from the formal garden to examine the huge private garden stretching southwards from the South Wing of the palace we find not the rigid contrivance of the garden to the north but a great naturalness.

The South Wing, possibly the residential range belonging to the owner, faced south across a colonnaded veranda to the sea. The excavation of 1967 showed that an artificial terrace existed, but it was not until 1969 that it became possible to examine the area in any detail. The land was divided between a modern building estate, a derelict chicken farm and a strip of pasture belonging to the Church Commissioners. At Easter 1969 trial trenches were dug within the chicken farm to test its potential while a careful watch was kept on the construction trenches opened on the building site. Under these rather unpromising conditions certain details of the Roman layout gradually came to light.

We now know that an artificial terrace was constructed for a distance of about 300ft south of the wing ending, at its south edge, on a quay wall of stone blocks and timber, beyond which lay the sea (**52**). How the sea water was retained in the huge lagoon-like inlet has not yet been defined, but some kind of mole built out across the harbour end may have kept the water back at low tide while the constant flow from the freshwater streams maintained the level. It is possible that lock gates were provided in the mole to allow ships to sail up to the terrace at high tide. This much is suggested by the construction of a channel 20ft wide dredged along the terrace edge. The intention was to provide a 5–6ft depth of water allowing quite large vessels to come close in.

The terrace itself, enclosed by a colonnade along the west side and probably also along

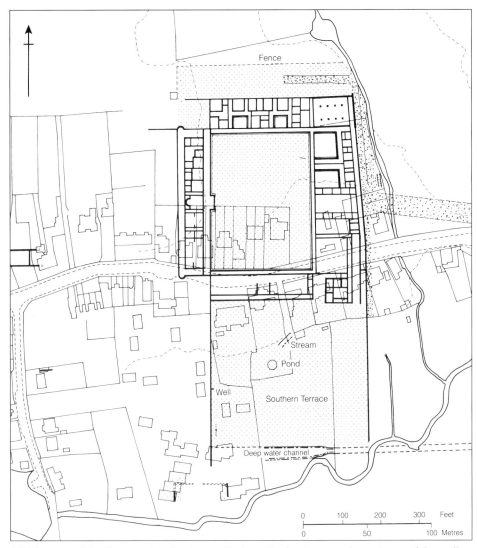

52 The extent of the Flavian palace showing the Southern Garden, its approaches and some of the ancillary buildings to the west

the east, seems to have been laid out as a 'natural' garden. At one point a shallow stream was found flowing into a large pond constructed towards the centre of the area. An artificial water supply was also piped into the western side of the garden, where there were no convenient natural springs to tap. Elsewhere the made-up surface is penetrated with short lengths of bedding trenches and isolated bedding pits, apparently laid out haphazardly, suggesting that shrubs and trees had been planted at random to produce the impression of gently sloping parkland leading down to the sea. The inlet at this point would have been about 400ft wide and on the opposite side the land sloped up again. Here careful tree planting could have contrived a superb enclosing landscape with wooded areas giving way gradually to a sea-shore. Even now, with all the modern development to which the area has been subjected, it is possible to recapture something of its former peaceful atmosphere.

There is still a lot to be learnt about this southern 'natural' garden. The rescue excavation identified a masonry structure about 100ft to the south-west of the garden. Could this have been a garden pavilion providing a distant view out to sea, or something more mundane like a warehouse? Future work may one day resolve the problem. The deep-water silts which clogged the lagoon after the garden was abandoned are of particular interest because under these waterlogged conditions organic material is preserved. Leather shoes, a wooden bowl and a wooden comb have been recovered, together with large quantities of pottery, some of it with food residues inside. Clearly, these layers offer the potential for learning about aspects of environment and life which, under normal archaeological conditions, are very seldom recoverable.

The palace, as we have so far described it, covered about 10 acres but it lay within a much larger complex which must have included estate buildings such as workshops, kitchens, store rooms and servants' quarters. Some idea of the layout is at last beginning to emerge. The palace was approached by a wide road leading due west from Chichester to the east front of the entrance hall, where it joined a service road, or street, which flanked the entire east façade of the building, running from the inlet north to beyond the front of the aisled hall. At this point the road turned at right-angles and ran through the centre of a fenced enclosure, north of the North Wing, to the general working yards west of the palace.

This northern enclosure, some 80ft wide, had been carefully levelled up with tips of gravel and clay at the time when the palace was laid out. Its northern limit was marked by a series of large fence posts which probably served as the basis of a close-boarded fence dividing the immediate territory of the palace from the land beyond. Levelling over the eastern part of the enclosure had raised the surface by 4–5ft above the valley floor. To the north where there was no make-up, a substantial marshy area formed, drained only by the canalized stream which ran along the eastern limit of the palace. With the marsh on the north, stream to the east and sea to the south, the palace would have looked impressively isolated.

Most of this northern enclosed area has not been extensively excavated but parts of several buildings are known to lie within. The western part of the enclosure, however, was totally examined before the present museum, concourse and service buildings were erected, and several interesting features have come to light. The angle between the North and West Wings was covered with a thickness of black soil containing churned-up occupation rubbish, suggesting the possibility of a well-manured garden. Kitchen gardens were a favourite adjunct to all private villas and houses in Italy and indeed have a much longer ancestry than the formal and decorative gardens which became popular only during the period of Hellenization in the first century BC. The kitchen garden was traditional to Rome. Here herbs were grown to flavour the food and flowers and plants were cultivated for offering to the gods on the household and public shrines. Quite probably this north-west corner of cultivated land at Fishbourne was the kitchen garden. We know that it was provided with a supply of fresh water led to the centre of the area by a wooden water-pipe joined to the aqueduct. Such a provision would have been essential to water the plants during the summer, when this part of the site would have dried out.

Close to the edge of the garden area was the base of a large masonry bread oven of the kind found in the bakery at Pompeii. It was a complex affair with air vents and raking channels at the bottom, and the main flue and oven chamber at a convenient working height above. An installation of this size would have been able to serve the needs of the entire palace. It was carefully situated close to the building it served, within easy reach of the road supplying it, near a water supply and not too far from the servants' quarters. Cart-loads of corn brought into the enclosure along the service road would have been off-loaded into storage buildings and ground into flour nearby. The exact site of the mill has not yet been identified but a massive grindstone of German lava was discovered here during building work. It was too large to have been rotated by hand and must therefore have come from a large establishment employing some form of simple machinery.

While baking was centralized in this northern enclosure, we do not yet know where the rest of the cooking was carried out. Fairly elaborate kitchens would have been needed to provide food for the banquets which must have been held in the palace and since no suitable accommodation has been found within the palace as it is now known, we must suppose that the kitchens as well as the servants' quarters lay somewhere to the west where contemporary foundations have been identified in limited trial excavations. This discovery raises the whole problem of the housing of the vast army of servants needed to maintain a building of this size. In addition to kitchens and servants' accommodation, there would probably have been provision for estate production and maintenance, storage facilities for raw materials and export commodities, in fact the entire administrative network required to run what must have been a considerable enterprise.

Finally we must turn to the area in front of the palace to the east, examined in a series of rescue excavations conducted with great energy and determination by Alec Down in 1983 and 1985–6. The work showed that much of the area immediately in front of the East Wing had been kept clear apart from the approach road leading to the entrance hall. A second road, probably a remetalled version of the north road of the pre-palace period, marked the north side of this open area. To the north of it was a palimpsest of bedding trenches, paths, gullies and rows of post-holes which evidently reflect cultivation over a considerable period of time. It is tempting to see this as an area set aside for productive market gardening along the approach to the palace. One of the discoveries of outstanding interest from this area were several 'planter' pots, ceramic vessels with holes in their sides and bases, which were used for the propagation of cuttings.

The approach to the palace must have been spectacular, the drive passing through an open grassy field flanked to the north by the rich gardens producing fruit and vegetables and to the south by the stream flowing in a shallow valley to the harbour, and there in front, looming magnificent, the low mass of the great building dominated by its huge and inspiring entrance hall. It was a contrived landscape carefully designed to communicate stability and opulence.

8. The owner and his changing fortunes

In the contemporary Romano-British countryside of the late first century there would have been nothing to compare with the great palace at Fishbourne. The average upper-class farmhouse, like those found at Lockleys and Park Street, were little bungalows of five or six rooms totalling no more than 60ft in length. Both of them together would have fitted into the courtyard in the East Wing. There were a few, more substantial, houses like the villas at Eccles in Kent, Angmering and the Fishbourne proto-palace, but these in no way compare to the size of the Flavian palace. By the middle of the fourth century larger establishments had grown up but even one of the largest, the villa at Woodchester in the Cotswolds, could have been fitted, courtyards and all, into the formal garden. Moreover these big fourth-century villas were usually the result of a gradual growth, sometimes beginning a century or two earlier, and included storage space and servants' quarters as well. The Fishbourne palace was planned and erected at one time.

Monumental masonry buildings were not, however, unknown in Britain in the late first century. In the Flavian period the country was in the throes of a massive programme of urban expansion. In many of the towns in the south large public buildings were being erected. In Cirencester and Verulamium the basilicas and fora are of this phase. So too is the first stage of the great religious centre in Bath with its temple to Sulis Minerva and the adjacent baths. In London there was a new palace probably put up for the provincial governor and nearer to Fishbourne, on Hayling Island, a long-established native temple was being rebuilt in fine masonry reminiscent of the palace. This remarkable phase of building activity is best seen in the context of a deliberate policy set in train by the Flavian governors to Romanize the province. When writing of the work of the governor Agricola, Tacitus is quite explicit: 'To induce a people hitherto scattered, uncivilised and therefore prone to fight, to grow pleasurably inured to peace and ease Agricola gave private encouragement and official assistance to the building of temples, forts and private villas ... And so the Britons were gradually led on to the amenities that make vice agreeable — arcades, baths and sumptuous banquets. They spoke of such novelties as civilisation when really they were only a feature of their enslavement.'

It was in the midst of this new-found enthusiasm for things Roman that the Fishbourne palace was built. But under whose authority? Governors might offer

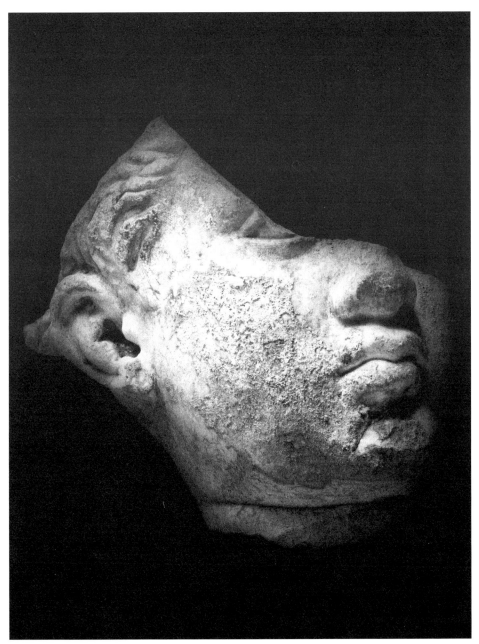

53 A marble head of a youth found in a late rubble deposit in the North Wing. The piece is of continental workmanship of late first-century date. The subject is a young man, originally wearing a metal helmet, with somewhat sullen features. It is a portrait study, in all probability of one of the owner's children

'private encouragement and official assistance' to those they favoured but to embark upon a project as ambitious as the building at Fishbourne implies a person of considerable power and wealth. Who was he — a high-ranking Roman official, a foreign speculator or a rich local landowner? In the absence of a building inscription to help us we will never know for certain but one person, Tiberius Claudius Togidubnus, stands out as a likely candidate. As a Roman citizen, a local client king and a long-standing friend of Rome his claims deserve to be taken seriously but first let us consider what can be deduced from the archaeological evidence.

The excavation has shown that after a brief military phase the site at Fishbourne began to develop a residential aspect with the building of a large, comfortable and well-appointed timber house, in use during the period c. AD 45–65. Some time in the early 60s the timber house was abandoned for a far more elaborate masonry building, the proto-palace, which incorporated a number of luxuries such as a bath suite and a colonnaded courtyard, and was elaborately decorated with *opus sectile* floors and painted walls. The proto-palace should be seen in the context of a number of rich houses that were being erected in the area at this time, at Angmering, Southwick, and probably also at Pulborough and Eastbourne. What distinguishes it is that it was only one element in a complex of masonry buildings under construction at Fishbourne in the Neronian and early Flavian period. Some time c. AD 75–80 the original scheme was abandoned and the palace was built incorporating the proto-palace in one corner. The evidence, as we have it, would suggest a degree of continuity in the ownership of the site with the residential facility being constantly upgraded.

Whilst these developments were in progress at Fishbourne the urban centre a mile or so away at Chichester was also enjoying a spate of building activity. Large areas were being developed with timber houses and with workshops producing fine pottery, bronzework and enamelling. Nearby more monumental structures were being erected. One inscription, dedicated to Nero in AD 58–60, was probably the base of an imperial statue. Another of about the same date, found just outside the Eastgate, was set up to the 'Mother Goddesses of the homeland' by a treasurer (*arcarius*) while the famous inscription from North Street records the erection of a temple to Neptune and Minerva for the well-being of the household of the emperor by Tiberius Claudius Togidubnus who is there given his title of 'great king of Britain'. The emperor is unnamed but is usually thought to be Nero though one of the later Flavian emperors, perhaps Titus, is also a possibility. We know little of the public buildings themselves but there is a strong possibility that an early public bath suite pre-dated the baths rebuilt in the early second century. Given this array of evidence it is not unreasonable to suggest that Togidubnus, the 'great king' may have been involved in encouraging the precocious development of his regional capital.

The palace built at Fishbourne in the late 70s was an exceptional structure which cannot be regarded simply as the centre of a rural estate. The plan gives some hint of how it may have functioned. Strictly it can be divided into three parts. The South Wing, with its view across the secluded southern gardens would have served as the private residential range while the North Wing and part of the East Wing were divided into apartments probably for visitors. The rest of the building — the imposing entrance hall, the formal garden, the West Wing raised on its high podium and the aisled hall — constituted the official, semi-public, part of the establishment the focus of which was

54 The Togidubnus inscription was unearthed in Chichester in 1723 and is now displayed on the wall of the Assembly Rooms. It records the erection of a temple to Neptune and Minerva by a guild of craftsmen, by permission of Tiberius Claudius Togidubnus, 'great king' of Britain

the audience chamber occupying the dominant central position in the West Wing. The plan of the building suggests, then, that the occupant was a person of wealth and exalted status who was expected to receive visitors in a manner reflecting that of the emperor himself and to provide hospitality and accommodation for his guests and their entourages.

Some further hints of the status of the palace come from items found from within and nearby. A fragment of the marble head of a youth (53), perhaps carved in Rome, appears to be a portrait study possibly of a child of the owner's family. A child's finger ring of gold was also found, inset with an oval intaglio of dark green plasma engraved with a bird. Gold rings are rare in Britain in the first century. At this time the wearing of such a ring was the privilege of someone of the equestrian order. The discovery of the ring in a level dating to the time of the proto-palace supports the view that the building was occupied by a family of exceptionally high rank. More recently another gold ring was found during excavations to the east of the palace. It was for an adult and was inscribed with the owner's name, *Ti Clavdi Catvari* — Tiberius Claudius Catuarus. The gold ring implies that Catuarus was also a man of equestrian rank who had been given Roman citizenship by Claudius or Nero. We now nothing more of him but can speculate that he was very probably a member of the British aristocracy sympathetic to the Roman cause and may even have been a kinsman of Togidubnus.

We have now sketched in the factual background relevant to the identity of the owner and it is time to confront the question could it have been Togidubnus? First let us rehearse what little is known or can reasonably be deduced of this shadowy figure. The facts are few. The Chichester inscription (54) gives his name Tiberius Claudius [T]ogidubnus and a title which may be read *rex magnus Brit*, 'great king of the Britons', while Tacitus, in his book *Agricola* tells us that 'certain states were given to Cogidubnus (he remained faithful down to our own times) according to an old and long accepted Roman tradition of using kings also as instruments for slavery' (Agricola XIV). Beyond these tantalizing scraps all is speculation.

We may begin with the reasonable assumption that Togidubnus was a member of the native British aristocracy — possibly of the Atrebatic royal house — at the time of the invasion of AD 43 and that he was allied to Rome. As we have already suggested it is even possible that he was brought up in Rome and returned to Britain with the invasion force to be installed as a client king of the Atrebates under Roman protection. At some stage he was given Roman citizenship, probably by the Emperor Claudius who showed a far-sighted concern for integrating worthy provincials into the government hierarchy and was accused for his efforts, in AD 48, of opening the ranks of the Senate to Gauls. Thereafter Togidubnus remained a loyal supporter of Rome, even throughout the Boudican rebellion of AD 60, and at some stage was given additional estates. When he died is unclear. Tacitus' remark could be taken to imply that Togidubnus was still in power as late as the 80s. There is nothing inherently unlikely in a person who was a young man of, say, 25 in AD 43 living to his 70s. A hint that he may have died about 80 is given by the presence in Britain, in the early 80s, of two very distinguished Roman lawyers. Men of such experience may have been needed to integrate the long-established client kingdom into the system of provincial government following the king's death. The possibility is worth noting though it proves nothing.

That the focus of Togidubnus' kingdom was the Chichester area seems reasonable. This was the centre of Atrebatic power in the pre-conquest period and the new Roman town was rapidly developing in the 50s and 60s, at least one building being erected under the patronage of the king. It is not unlikely therefore that his residence lay somewhere nearby — where more appropriate than at Fishbourne? The structural progression we have identified at Fishbourne could well reflect the increasing status and wealth of the king — a timber house of the 50s replaced by the proto-palace in the mid 60s which was in turn absorbed into the great palatial building of the late 70s. Could it be that each new building project reflects the reward of a particular act of loyalty to the authorities, the proto-palace following his support during the disastrous year of the Boudican rebellion and the main palace erected in the aftermath of the Year of the Four Emperors (AD 69) when the Empire was thrown into turmoil on the death of Nero, and Vespasian emerged triumphant? In Britain the legions were not heavily involved in the struggle but they tended to favour Vitellius. It is not unlikely that Togidubnus, who would surely have known Vespasian as a young commander in AD 43, lent his support to the future emperor, perhaps significantly swaying the opinion of the civil population.

All this is, and will remain, speculation. We are most unlikely ever to know for certain who owned Fishbourne. A case can be made out for Togidubnus but it is essentially a case based on possibilities. All that can safely be said is that it is simpler, on present evidence, to argue that Togidubnus was the owner than that he was not.

9. The second century

Throughout the second and third centuries changes, sometimes minor sometimes sweeping, can be detected in the structure of the old palace. Gradually as time went on less and less attention was paid to the West, East and South Wings and all the effort went into improving the inhabited area, which by the third century centred upon the west end of the North Wing.

The first major change came at the beginning of the second century, when the aisled hall was modified and a bath suite was inserted into the passageway between the hall and the east end of the North Wing (55). Why such an addition should have been required is difficult to say, because the south-east baths were probably still in good working order. One possibility is that the palace was now divided between two owners, each requiring their own baths but it could be that the southern part of the old palace had become uncongenial because of the high water-table and nearby marsh. At any event the new baths were built.

The plan was quite simple; the passageway was divided into three by cross partitions. The northern room, the *caldarium*, was fitted with a hypocaust chamber beneath a mortar floor supported on piles of tiles. The heat was provided by hot air warmed up in a stokery immediately outside the east wall. The masonry sides to the flue still survive, projecting for some 4ft, showing that they would originally have supported a large boiler of bronze so that the fire beneath would also have heated the water needed by the bathers. Such economy was a common feature in Roman bath-houses.

The middle room, the *tepidarium*, derived its hot air second-hand from the *caldarium* hypocaust and was therefore of a lower temperature. A small plunge bath, just large enough to sit comfortably in, was built in a recess opening from the centre of the west wall. It was floored with tiles and its walls were rendered with a waterproof red mortar. Here in the warm congenial atmosphere the owner and his friends must have spent many a relaxed afternoon.

The third room, to the south, was provided with a central drain made of gutter blocks removed from the old palace gardens. Since the rest of the details have been destroyed, it is impossible to reconstruct much of the original state of the room, but in all probability it was the cold room (*frigidarium*) where, after some time in the warmth of the other rooms, the pores could be closed with a dousing of cold water before one emerged into the chilling open air. An alternative is that the *frigidarium* was built in the

The second century

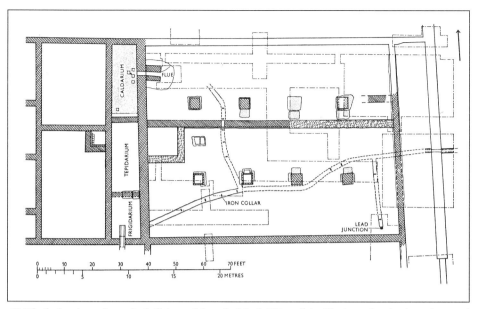

55 *The bath suite and exercise hall inserted into the North Wing of the Flavian palace in the early second century*

now much ruined room which projected east from the *tepidarium* and that the room with the open drain was a latrine. The evidence is not sufficient to be conclusive.

The new bath suite was, then, modest but comfortable. Its walls were all carefully plastered and painted with a deep red dado and white panels above, the panels being defined by red bands and outlined with concentric orange frame-lines. Above was a 'cornice moulding' painted in graded tones of red. The window embrasures and doorways were also plastered and painted with their angles and splays picked out in red. All three rooms employed this basic decor but the *tepidarium* in addition included some black and yellow areas and panels of white splashed with red and yellow.

The bath suite required an efficient water supply. This was provided by a series of wooden water-pipes — lengths of timber hollowed out and jointed together with collars of iron — which were laid in trenches cut through the floor of the aisled hall. The timber has rotted but it was possible to trace the trenches in which the pipes had been laid and to locate the iron collars used to join the sections. By this means it could be shown that the main pipe led in from the east, twisting between the piers of the hall and ending up in the vicinity of the southern room. Two subsidiary pipes branched off, one running north to the hot water boiler over the *caldarium* flue, the other running to the south-east corner of the hall where it ended with a lead junction box leading to a vertical lead pipe, which would have served a drinking fountain or basin. The way in which the main pipe twisted around the piers suggests that they were still standing at this time, but the northern branch pipe passed neatly through a hole which had been carefully constructed in a new wall built right across the hall from one end to the other on very substantial rubble footings cut through the original floor. The conclusion therefore must be that at the time when the water-pipes were laid, or at least were still functioning, the hall was reduced in width from 66ft to 38ft, the original southern row of piers now serving as the central supports for the roof of the redesigned structure. The area to the north seems now to have become a working yard from which the flue could be stoked and in which the fuel supply for the baths was housed. The reduction of the hall is interesting because it implies that its original use, as a place of assembly, was now over, the early second-century house no longer needing such a building. Why reconstruction was necessary is not clear, but after 20–30 years the roof timbers may have been beginning to give way under the enormous weight of the roof. The rebuilding was, however, in a good style of masonry and was designed to make maximum use of existing structures and material: the new north wall was probably built entirely from the stone dismantled from the original north wall, while the reduced width of the building would have allowed the original roof timbers to be used even if rotten ends had to be sawn off.

A great deal of trouble had been taken to reconstitute the hall but what function did it now serve? The most reasonable explanation is that it became an exercise hall belonging to the baths. Halls for this purpose were a common adjunct to Roman bathing suites — here one could play games and take exercise before bathing. The small drinking fountain constructed at this time in the corner of the hall would have been an acceptable facility in such an arrangement. As we will see later, the hall may have continued in this function long after the North Wing baths were demolished.

The other late first- or early second-century alterations to the palace were relatively insignificant structurally but of no less interest. In room N13, in the centre of the North Wing, a remarkable new mosaic was laid over the partly destroyed earlier floor (**56–7; Col 22**). It was of a complex design consisting of a central roundel enclosing a Medusa head simply drawn in black, red and yellow, with a great mat of hair interwoven with writhing yellow-eyed snakes. The Medusa panel was set in a square surrounded by eight octagonal panels, each enclosing a different type of flower, leaf or rosette. These panels were retained within an overall square frame with the corners filled in with simple chequer-board designs. One of these had been laid incorrectly to have one extra row of squares – this meant that there was not enough room to enclose the adjacent octagon with its correct double border, and even the rosette inside had to be jammed up. This is only one of the numerous small errors which are apparent in the design. The outer borders were composed of multiple bands of different motifs of which the most amusing is of white circles with little pointed tails inside, clearly meant to be a copy of the tendril borders of the West Wing mosaics. The whole floor is extremely lively and crammed with pattern but the technical skill of its mosaicist was low; not only were mistakes made in the basic design but the choice and blend of colours was crude. One is forced to the conclusion that it was laid with great enthusiasm by someone with little or no experience, copying what he liked from the mosaics around and making up the rest.

Some indication of the date of the floor is provided by small pieces of samian pottery which had been cut up to form red tesserae used in the main design. Expert opinion has concluded that no piece dating to after AD 90–100 was used. This, as we will see, contrasts noticeably with other later mosaics in the building which contain only pottery of mid to late second-century date. It looks then as though the mosaicist was using pottery currently in use, and that as a method for dating the floors there is some internal consistency about it. On stylistic grounds and on the basis of the samian *tesserae*,

The second century

56 The Medusa mosaic inserted into room N13 in the early second century. The stippled area has been destroyed by ploughing

therefore, a date somewhere about or a little before AD 100 is indicated. This is of particular interest because it strongly suggests that we are looking at one of the first attempts by local craftsmen at mosaic art in this country. The earlier mosaics of the Flavian period were all laid by continentals; here surely are the first faltering steps of a local. It is tempting to see in the great profusion of design something of the underlying feeling behind native Celtic art.

One other alteration might perhaps belong to this early period, the construction of a corridor along the west side of the North Wing, to link the rooms and corridors of the North Wing to those of the West without one having to go outside the building and use the original colonnades. The new corridor was floored with a simple red tessellated floor with a chequer-board design picked out with grey-brown *tesserae*. The design is interesting since it incorporates the same ideas as those behind the earlier mosaic in

57 The Medusa mosaic in room N13 as originally found, a large area having been destroyed by ploughing. The workmanship was somewhat uneven and several mistakes were made in the layout, as will be appreciated in fig 56

room W6 — some areas are shown as grey on red, others as red on grey. This simple type of reversal pattern was in use in Italy in the late first and early second centuries but does not seem to have remained in fashion long. The construction of the corridor facilitated the movement between one wing and the other; it also bypassed the northwest corner of the garden which at this time had begun to be used as a tip for kitchen refuse.

The first series of alterations to the palace imply that certain important social changes had taken place; the assembly hall was no longer required, the formal garden was beginning to go out of use — both facts strongly suggest that the official/semi-public functions were now at an end. But this does not mean decline, far from it. The bath suite and exercise hall and the new mosaics were luxuries which very few contemporary landowners could afford. Changes there may have been but the quality of domestic life was still high.

The middle of the second century saw the first major reformation of the old building. The main difficulty in understanding the period is in assessing the order in which the alterations took place and indeed whether they were part of a single cohesive policy of rebuilding planned at one time, or a series of rebuildings undertaken haphazardly over a period. The archaeological evidence does not allow such fine distinctions to be made but viewing the changes in terms of the overall results it would appear that the builders were working towards a definite preconceived plan.

The most drastic of the alterations was the demolition of the east end of the North Wing, including the relatively new bath suite. The whole of the superstructure from the west end of the hall to the east end of room N15 was removed down to the footings and the building materials carted off for reuse elsewhere, leaving only loose mortar and chips of stone and tile to be spread out over the old mosaics, several of which miraculously still survived the demolition and were buried. The whole of the colonnaded east courtyard was also pulled down and the rather ragged east end of the North Wing thus exposed was tidied up with a length of wall which created a new corridor and room. There is some evidence to suggest that the old south wall of the wing was retained, linking what was left of the North Wing to the hall.

The reason why these far-reaching demolitions were carried out was simple. The east end of the North Wing had been built over the remains of an early timber building and a number of drainage ditches filled with loose silty soil. Although the palace footings were substantial enough to remain unaffected, serious subsidence soon began with the result that the colonnades and the floors started to contort and slump. This was no doubt a gradual process but by the middle of the second century, 60 or 70 years after the initial building, things had become serious — the subsidence of the mosaic in room N21 shows how bad it was — and the decision to demolish was taken. The demolition meant that the North Wing baths were removed leaving, incidentally, a coin of Hadrian (AD 117–38) in the last lot of ash which they had not bothered to rake out of the flue.

The replacement baths, built on a larger scale, were inserted into the courtyard of the East Wing, as close as possible to the hall which presumably continued to function as the exercise hall for the bathers (**58–60**). The basis of the new arrangement was simple: the old colonnade was pulled down and a new wall was built right across the courtyard from east to west which, together with the standing walls, created an enclosure 70ft by 55ft; within this the baths were built. The old stylobate on the south and east sides of the courtyard was used as the basis for new walls, and a series of cross walls were built dividing up the veranda into two ranges of rooms, into which the baths were inserted. The south range was not used directly for bathing purposes.

The *caldarium* was a small affair, a little under 10ft square. It was floored in two parts; the northern part was raised on a pillared hypocaust while the southern, at a lower level, was covered with a plain red tessellated floor which sloped to a drain in the west wall. The tessellated area was the floor of a hot plunge bath set in the south side of a normally heated *caldarium*. The supply of hot air and water was provided by a stokery outside the east wall, towards which the line of a wooden pipe could be traced taking water to a tank, possibly built on the masonry platform created just east of the flue. From here it would have been fed, as required, into the hot water boiler — a simple but effective system.

Immediately to the north lay the *tepidarium*, a long room with an apsidal bath built in a recess in its east wall. The heat for the main room was provided by the hot air passing into a series of channels below the floor, linked to the hypocaust of the *caldarium*. Although the sub-floor structures have suffered considerably from robbing, enough survives to show that the arrangement was very carefully thought out. As the plan shows, the air entered through two vents in the dividing wall passing into two wide channels divided by walls of horizontally set box tiles and then into the central channels not directly linked to the *caldarium*, thus ensuring an even heat. Along the east wall the box tiles were set closely together and linked to similar tiles set vertically so as to form an internal hollow jacketing to the wall. In this way the hot air, having circulated beneath the floor, passed into the vertical ducts rising naturally until it was expelled through chimneys set along the top of the wall or in the roof. The small apsidal bath was provided with a subsidiary source of heat by means of a separate stokery, above which would have been its hot water boiler. The waste water from this little bath seems to have

The second century

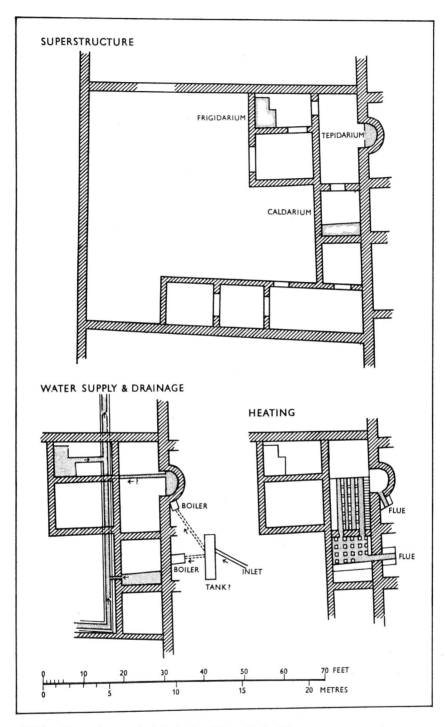

58 The mid second-century baths in the East Wing with the different systems separated out

The second century

59 and 60 In the East Wing of the palace lay a large colonnaded courtyard surrounded on three sides by a stylobate of limestone blocks, which originally supported the columns of the colonnade. In front of the stylobate was a ground-level gutter to collect rain-water. The gutter led to the north-east corner of the garden, where it opened into a culvert running beneath the veranda floor. In the second century the columns were pulled down and the old veranda was partitioned off and turned into a bath suite. [ ] is shown part of the pillared hypocaust of the caldarium *with the tessellated floor of the hot plunge bath beyond*

flowed through a drain set below the floor and then into the old stylobate gutter. This sub-floor drain, though not apparent within the room, marked the north side of the hypocaust system and therefore divided the room into two parts, a southern heated part and a northern cooler section. This type of graded atmosphere is a sophistication seldom met with in small private bathing establishments of this kind.

Next to the *tepidarium* lay the *frigidarium*, a long room with a sunken cold plunge bath in one end (**61**). The bath was floored with reused tiles and slabs of marble set in a hard waterproof cement. In one corner a bench was provided joined to a ledge running along the north wall so that the bathers could sit between plunges with their legs dangling into the water. The benches and the walls of the rooms were coated with a thick layer of waterproof pink mortar. Waste water was removed by means of a substantial tile-built culvert which ran beneath the floor of the rest of the *frigidarium* and emptied into the stylobate gutter. The arrangement suggests that the floor of this part of the room would have been of timber laid above the culvert and the old gutter.

In the angle between the *caldarium* and the *tepidarium* lay another room which probably served as an undressing room (*apodyterium*). In this position it would have been a general concourse as well. From here a bather could choose whether to go into the cold plunge or begin his treatment in the more normal way by going into the *tepidarium*, followed by the *caldarium* and finishing off with a cold plunge.

The superstructure of the suite can be reconstructed within limits (**62**). It is almost certain that the heated rooms were roofed with a vault running north–south from the south wall of the *caldarium* to the north wall of the *tepidarium* — normal architectural

61 The second-century bath suite, built into the East Wing of the palace, possessed a substantial cold swimming bath, shown here. The masonry of the walls has been robbed away but the floor, of reused tile and slabs of marble, is well preserved. In one corner and along one wall was a bench to allow the bather to sit with feet dangling in the water

62 Suggested reconstruction of the mid-second-century baths (by Nigel Sunter)

procedure would have demanded it and several blocks of tufa, a light stone frequently used in vaults were found in the rubble. The *frigidarium* and *apodyterium* were probably protected by a single pitched roof clad with tiles, while the south range may have been given a lean-to roof along the same lines as the original veranda. It is more difficult to say how the rooms of the old East Wing fared, for while the two stokeries built in them would have required some form of roofing to keep off the rain it is most unlikely that much of the original roof remained, not the least because of the problem of ventilation required by the presence of the flues.

Internally, all the walls of the main rooms of the baths were plastered and painted, the best evidence of the general decor coming from the masses of plaster which choked the cold plunge bath. Here, it can be shown, the walls were painted with a deep red dado $3\frac{1}{2}$–4ft high with white walls above divided into panels, each enlivened with a concentric black frame-line. The *tepidarium*, however, was far more elaborately decorated with areas painted to represent marble, one in grey splashed with red, black and yellow, another in red splashed with black, both probably serving as part of the dado. Above was some form of elaborate panelling which included bands of bright blue, black and white, but of this upper area little survives.

The drainage system has already been referred to in passing but it deserves a more detailed consideration because of the ingenious way in which the old gutter of the Flavian garden was retained and modified. The three drains from the *caldarium*, *tepidarium* and cold plunge all lead towards the gutter and must originally have emptied directly into it. The *caldarium* drain was composed of two ceramic water-pipes (probably robbed from the garden), placed together so as to form a V-bend, a refinement clearly designed to remove the risk of draughts which would have detracted from the comfort of the hot bath. The drain from the much larger cold plunge was necessarily of a more

The second century

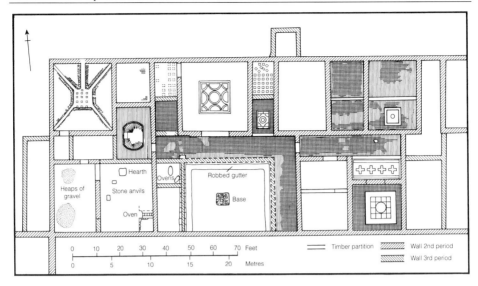

63 The west end of the North Wing, showing all the second- and third-century alterations

considerable cross section, otherwise it would have taken inordinately long for the bath to empty: since draughts were less of a problem here no traps were devised. The third drain, from the *tepidarium*, has been so completely destroyed that nothing can be said of its form. A considerable volume of water would have come from the baths while they were in use, all of it flowing beneath the timber floors of the *frigidarium* and *apodyterium* and into the tile-built culvert through which the waste eventually passed out of the building.

Somewhere in this complex would have been the latrines placed, presumably, downstream from the baths themselves. The most likely position is the recess at the end of the corridor which passed along the north end of the old Flavian east range, exactly over the tile-built culvert. Here, it appears, the sides of the old drain were removed down to its base and two revetting walls were built across so that a sump was formed linked directly to the outfall. The water flowing from the baths would have built up behind one of the walls and flowed over, flushing out the sump while at the same time the wall prevented a flow-back from the sump towards the baths. Thus by this simple series of alterations a highly effective drainage system was created for a latrine. The flooring and seating above, which here would have been constructed in timber, have left no trace because all the surrounding masonry superstructure has been robbed to the footings.

It will be seen from the foregoing description that the new bath suite, built in the middle of the second century to replace the demolished North Wing baths, was well-planned, comfortable and rather more spacious than its predecessor. These baths alone suggest a rise in affluence of the owner, a suggestion which is dramatically borne out by the nature of the alterations to the inhabited part of the North Wing.

As we have described above, the eastern part of the North Wing had, by the middle of the second century, become unsafe through subsidence and was demolished. The western part of the wing, however, continued in active use and it was at about this time that a series of alterations were made to convert the old structure into a more

The second century

64 A general view of the west end of the North Wing, showing the arrangement towards the end of the third century, by which time the palace had reached its final form. The latest alteration to be made was the addition of a heating system to the corner room. Excavation showed that the heating arrangements were never used and were apparently unfinished. In the adjacent room is the Shell (or Peacock) mosaic. To the left the Flavian mosaics remain though in a very patched state

manageable unit (**63; Col 3–4**). Of primary importance was the creation of an improved system of communications. This was achieved by adding a new L-shaped corridor to the eastern end of the reconstituted structure and linking it to another corridor made by dividing room N14. Thus it was possible to move freely from the east end to the courtyard which was retained as an essential part of the design. At the west end (**64**), room N5 was divided into three parts, one was added to room N4, the original dividing wall now being removed, the second part was floored with a new mosaic pavement and the third became a corridor linking the mosaic room to the tessellated corridor to the west.

It was probably at this time that a number of the large rooms were divided by timber partitions. Room N12 was made into two in this way. The northern part, provided with a new plaster moulding at the junction of the walls and floor, was kept up in style while the southern part eventually became some kind of store room. Rooms N10 and 11 were also divided by timber walls, both halves of each now being refloored with red tesserae. The southern half of room N11 was also provided with a small patterned mosaic panel. Room N9 on the other hand was retained but refloored with *opus signinum* (a hard mortar containing crushed brick). The southern part of room N14, of which the northern side was cut off to become a corridor, was refloored with a black and white

The second century

65 The floor in room N14 was relaid during the second century in a style closely similar to the Flavian mosaic in room N12. This conscious copying implies that the pattern was still acceptable to the later occupants

mosaic very much in the style of the Flavian floor in room N12 (**65**). While it could have been a direct copy it is more likely that the second-century mosaicist simply relaid, in a rather less competent fashion, the mosaic already there.

The renovated building was now provided with two small heated rooms on either side of room N7, both of which were constructed by dividing off the two corridors, N6 and 8, from the colonnade and cutting them into two almost equal halves. In the northern halves hypocausts were inserted beneath mortar floors, while the hot air needed to heat them was produced by stokeries constructed in the southern halves. This rather peculiar arrangement was necessitated partly by the existing structures into which things had to be fitted, and partly because it seems that the building now fronted north onto the original service road and to have put the flues outside the north walls of the rooms would have detracted from the northern aspect of the building.

In addition to the purely structural changes, the reconstituted building was provided with four new mosaics, of which the finest was laid in room N7 which now seems to have become the principal room (**66; Col 19**). The patterned panel in the centre of the room was a lively polychrome arrangement in which black and white were dominant but various tones of red and yellow were also used. The centre of the floor, a roundel enclosed within a competently drawn braided guilloche, depicted a winged Cupid sitting astride a dolphin and holding its reins in one hand and a trident in the other (**Col 21**). While the drawing and shading have a certain lively quality, especially the body muscles which are particularly well conceived, the strange outlining of the figure in black has ruined the effect of the curly hair and has made the hands into rather

The second century

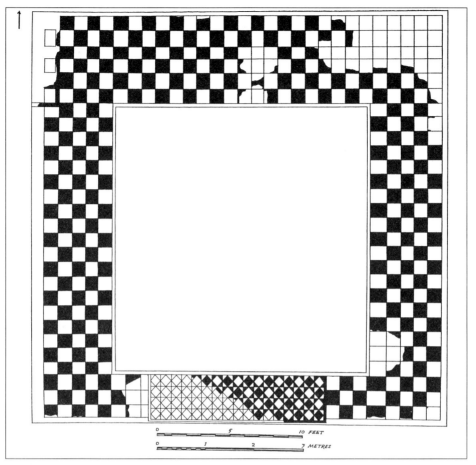

66 The border of the Cupid mosaic in room N7. The central square contains the patterned and figured mosaics shown in colour plate .

amorphous shapes. The spacing of the figure within the circle, always a difficult thing to get right, is also unhappy and to deflect the eye from the large area of white in the lower half stylized rocks have been drawn.

The centre roundel is supported within a square panel by four semicircular panels and four quadrants. The semicircles each contain a fabulous sea beast paired with the one on the opposite side of the floor, two being sea panthers and two sea-horses (**67–8; Col 20**). The sea panthers are carefully drawn in yellow, red, black and white, both copying the same basic features but with minor variations: the western beast has claws and fangs while his partner is of a much more docile appearance. The difference may have been deliberately contrived to represent male and female. The two sea-horses are predominantly black with details picked out in white and with red tongues. The workmanship of the southern beast is brilliantly assured, the proportions, the stance and the contortions of his tail are all perfectly controlled. His opposite number is much less happy, a poor emaciated ill-conceived thing, surely the work of a less skilled craftsman. The sea beasts and the shell-like quadrants are retained in simple borders of twisted

67, 68 The two sea-horses from the Cupid mosaic

69 A cantharos from the Cupid mosaic

The second century

70 Part of the border of the Cupid mosaic showing a bird perched on a leaf – possibly the 'signature' of the mosaicist

guilloche. The hollow square spaces between the panels were basically white with large vases in black almost filling them (**69**). Each vase is different and each has curly handles turning into tendrils and tendrils growing out of the bases — a common technique for filling up awkward spaces.

The design so far described was retained within a square border of twisted guilloche, not without interest for it shows two distinct styles of workmanship. The northern part was rather less ambitious in choice of colour but the mosaicist was practised at making the guilloche turn corners. The southern part was more varied in colour range but the corners were incompetently handled. Again, then, we have evidence of the work of different people. A further point of interest is that no attempt was made to integrate the guilloche of the enclosed panels with that of the border as was the normal practice later — lack of basic skill, or at least lack of planning, may be the explanation. Outside the guilloche were two further bands of border, one showing triangles arranged base to apex and the outer one depicting central vases supported by simple tendril scrolls. Again an examination of the detail shows both a general lack of fine planning and variations which might well result from the work of different craftsmen. Perhaps the most interesting single detail is on the north side, on the third leaf west from the central vase. Here the mosaicist has twisted the stem in such a way as to leave space for a small black bird (**70**). Maybe this is simply a defiant gesture against boredom but another possibility is that it is his signature.

The evidence from the samian *tesserae* included within the floor suggests a date after about AD 160 for its construction. Stylistically this date would be perfectly acceptable, allowing the floor to be placed at the beginning of one of the well-defined local schools of craftsmanship, which were growing up in this country as a response to the demands of a society becoming increasingly affluent under Roman rule. While the Dolphin floor is a great advance on the Medusa mosaic, it still shows a faltering uncertainty in construction, which adds considerably to its interest and visual impact.

The patterned panel was set within a surround composed of alternating squares of black and white, another feature harking back to the earlier traditions of the Flavian period (**66**). In front of the south side of the floor the pattern becomes more complex, incorporating a square-set-within-square design. This was, in effect, a 'mat' laid to enliven the main entrance to the room, running the full width of the wide south doorway. The door itself was made more impressive by flanking pilasters which can still be traced in the surviving footings. Between these a flight of wooden steps led up from the colonnade to the floor of the room, which was at a higher level. The patterning of the surround also suggests that a door led out of the north-west corner into the little heated room next door.

The reflooring of the room is most unlikely to have been the only change in decor: in all probability the walls were repainted at the same time. A quantity of wall plaster has been recovered, giving some idea of the fine quality of the work though the individual pieces are too small to allow large-scale reconstruction. The general arrangement was not unlike the Flavian style of inlaid marbles but the quality of the brushwork and choice of colour-range differed. The 'marbles' used included a deep purple with a coarse graining picked out in blue, a pale purple with textures in blue, red and grey, and a dark red backing painted with a curvilinear graining in green and blue. The strip 'marbles' and 'mouldings' were predominantly of black, white and bright blue in various combinations. Another part of the room seems to have been provided with niches painted in white with dangling frills of bright red outlined and enlivened with green. Exactly where in the room this came from we cannot be sure, but one possibility is that the curved plaster does not represent the lining of niches but is, in fact, part of the ceiling painting.

The large room in the corner of the wing, room N1, does not appear to have been refloored at this time unless a thin discontinuous lens of mortar which survives represents the basal levels of a mosaic, since removed by the construction of a hypocaust late in the third century. At any event the walls were replastered and painted, as can be shown by the relationship of the base of the painting to a floor level between the original Flavian mosaic and the late third-century hypocaust. A large area of plaster survived in position on the west side of the room, showing that the room was provided with a skirting of deep purple-red followed by a strip of pink painted with purple flowers. Above this was a further horizontal strip in a deep green forming the outermost border of the main wall panels, which here were painted in pale green with designs incorporating pink and white flowers and stripes of other colours. Lying loose in the rubbish of the room were fragments from different designs, including free-hand brown and blue painting and areas of yellow splashed with a red-brown. The style is totally different from the Flavian work but there are several similarities, both in the range of colours and the quality of the brushwork, which suggest a close relationship with the more elaborate painting in room N7.

The new room created when N5 was chopped up was no less impressive. It was provided with a most unusual mosaic pavement which included a central rectangular element with two apsidal-ended panels, divided into multicoloured rays, attached to each of its long sides (**Col 23**). The design is difficult to interpret because a substantial part of the central area has been destroyed, but we believed that it depicted the tails of two fish, the rest of which had been dug away by a later pit. If this were so then the semicircular rayed panels were probably scallop shells like the famous mosaic depicting a large shell found in the Roman town of Verulamium (St Albans). For a long time we referred to the floor as the Shell mosaic but during the period when the remains were being consolidated we became aware that the Italian mosaicists regrouting the floor were referring to it as the Peacock mosaic: the reason was soon apparent. Viewed from the west the two 'fish tails' look very much like the knobbly legs of a bird the 'tails' being the feet and what was considered to be a fin could well be a spur. If this is so then the 'shells' can be envisaged as the opened up tail of a peacock. Which interpretation is preferred may be left to the viewer.

Room N2, to the north, was provided with a mosaic pavement at this stage but very little survives except for the edge of a panel and a chequer-board pattern of black and white squares. The other rooms at the west end of the North Wing all retained their original Flavian mosaics, which continued to be heavily used and patched whenever holes appeared.

The fourth mosaic assignable to the middle of the second century was laid in the southern half of the divided room N11, as a small multicoloured panel in the middle of a plain red tessellated floor (**Col 24**). It consisted quite simply of a central rosette surrounded by a complex and rather inconsistent fret pattern which in turn was enclosed within a border of coloured cushion-shaped lenses arranged diagonally.

The second century

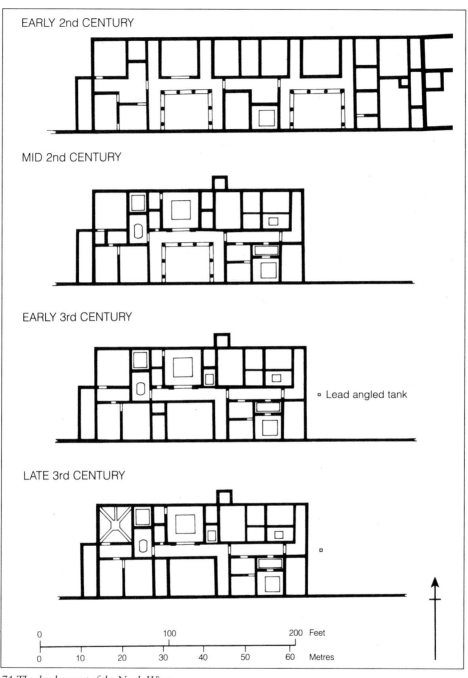

71 The development of the North Wing

Although the floor was simple and unassuming it would have provided a centre of interest in the room, suggesting that it may have served as an ante-room to its northern half where furniture and fittings would have relieved the need for patterned floors.

In the south-west corner of the wing rooms N3 and the enlarged N4 appear to have been used as work rooms and perhaps for storage, but whether this began in the second century or later cannot be determined. Room N4 was fitted with an oven inserted into the south-east corner and represented now only by its flue, but the basic structure was of considerable proportions and it could well have served as the bakery replacing the detached Flavian bakery which had gone out of use by the early second century. A small hearth was built in the northern part of the room at about this time, but no particular function can be assigned to it. Finally two large blocks of stone were found on the floor with their upper surfaces very worn as the result of a pounding or hammering process. The fittings are appropriate to a kitchen.

An examination of the immediate environment of the reconstituted North Wing shows that to the west, south-west and east thick layers of black occupation rubbish began to accumulate. This does not necessarily imply that middens were allowed to form close to the building, such squalor would hardly have been allowed at the time when the building was so rapidly developing. It is far more reasonable to interpret this material as the direct result of the deliberate manuring of gardens around the building with kitchen refuse. The abraded nature of the potsherds tends to support the view that the ground had been well dug over. Immediately outside the new east end of the wing a wooden tank, possibly for water, had been set into the ground; while the wood has rotted the internal angle bindings of lead and the large-headed iron tacks which held them in place still survived in position.

The north side of the building was, as we have mentioned above, its front, looking out upon the Flavian enclosure, a made-up area crossed by a metalled road linked directly to the north–south service road. At least one forward projecting addition was made to the building at this time, attached to the north wall of room N9. Its function is unclear unless it served as a porch. The area around it had been metalled with compacted gravel in a manner suitable for an entrance path. The excavation of this area has been limited and further details are lacking.

During the first 60 years of the second century the old palace was altered out of all recognition. From a vast semi-public residence set in splendid landscaped surroundings it was transformed into a smaller, and no doubt far more comfortable, villa concentrated in the west part of the North Wing with a detached bath suite inserted into the old East Wing. How much demolition of obsolete structures took place during this time it is impossible to say. Parts of the North and East Wings were certainly razed (**71**) but, as we will see in the next chapter, much of the West Wing probably remained in a roofed state, and for a while the old entrance hall in the East Wing continued to be used. Of the southern part of the palace we are entirely ignorant. The absence of second- and third-century finds from the admittedly limited excavation might suggest that this part of the site was no longer occupied. One interesting detail is that a fence was constructed at some post-Flavian date across the garden more or less along the line of the north side of the central path, some of the posts cutting into the now disused bedding trenches. The fence is otherwise undated but its close relationship to the axis of the building suggests a Roman date. It could be the southern boundary fence of the second-century building dividing the occupied area from the abandoned and demolished southern side.

While the building had been drastically reduced in size, and strictly can no longer be considered as a palace, the standard of living was still remarkably high. Far from existing in a parasitic fashion on the luxuries of the past, its owners had constructed within the shell of the old structure a new villa, geared to a smaller establishment and to the domestic needs of a single family, in a style still exceptional in the contemporary countryside. Few second-, or even early third-, century villas could boast four new polychrome mosaics and a bath suite. Who the second-century owners were we will never know — perhaps they were the family of the original owner, unable to keep up the standards of the past, but it could equally be that the estates had been sold off to the *nouveaux riches*. It is one of the many intriguing questions which must remain unanswered.

10. The third century

Throughout most of the third century the inhabited part of the North Wing was subjected to changes, usually of a relatively minor nature, which maintained and improved slightly the standard of living without dramatically altering the structure. To begin with the little hypocaust rooms on either side of room N7 proved awkward to work: the flues would have belched smoke into the rest of the building and supplies of fuel had to be carried into the centre of the inhabited structure. Clearly this was all highly unsatisfactory. Early in the third century therefore they ceased to be heated and the southern parts of the elongated passage which had housed the stokeries were levelled up and new floors were laid, a plain red tessellated floor in room N6 and a small mosaic surrounded by a tessellated border in N8. The reflooring in room N6 was particularly interesting because beneath it, in the ash and rubble levelled up to form its foundation, a silver denarius of the Emperor Septimius Severus was found. The coin was of a type issued in 196–7 and since it was only slightly worn it cannot have been in circulation for long. The floor above it is therefore unlikely to date much after the early years of the third century. The mosaic in room N8, which in all probability is part of the same series of alterations, may therefore be assigned to the same date.

The mosaic is of an interesting but straightforward design (**Col 25**). In the centre is a complex knot motif enclosed within a circle of braided guilloche which floats on a plain white background supported on four sides by pairs of dolphins facing centrally-placed vases. All this is set within a square frame, with shell motifs in the corners, and with additional panels containing diamonds at each end. The room seems to have been divided by a timber partition from the veranda to the south. The floor is too simple to enable much to be said of its stylistic affinities except that an early third-century date would be acceptable. Its interest lies mainly in the relative sterility of the competently executed pattern. The mosaicists available in the early third century at Fishbourne were not as able as those practising half a century earlier.

At the time of these refloorings alterations were made to the courtyard immediately to the south (**72**). Until then it seems that the original colonnade had been retained with its gutter still functioning to carry off the rain-water. Now, however, the columns were removed and their place taken along the north and east sides by dwarf walls, probably with some kind of balustrade supporting the veranda roof. The north and east sides of the veranda were then floored with red tessellation. Although the dwarf wall and the

The third century

72 *The west courtyard in the North Wing seen after total excavation and the erection of the cover building but before conservation*

original stylobate blocks upon which it was built have been robbed away, much of the tessellated floor remains in position at such a level that the wall must have been built to revet its outer edge, since the stylobate blocks would have been too low. The veranda floor can be shown to be of early third-century date because it was laid in one with the tessellated surround to the mosaic in room N8. The improvement to the courtyard, which really amounted to partially closing it in, was a logical follow-up to the abandonment of the stokeries: the whole of this south side was now linked closely together as a single unit.

At this time the western arm of the veranda was completely walled in to form a pair of work rooms, one of which was provided with a small oven. This new unit, together with the rooms to the west, N3 and 4, comprised the work rooms and kitchens of the building, neatly tucked away in one corner, the rest of the inhabited part of the building forming an L-shape.

The reconstruction of the veranda turned it into a linking corridor as opposed to a place from which the enclosed garden could be viewed, the old garden now serving more as a light-well than an integral part of the landscaping. It is probably at about this time that a massive concrete foundation was laid within the garden, measuring about 6ft square and nearly 2ft deep, and built of layers of greensand rubble interleaved with thick spreads of pink mortar. The top of the foundation, which was level with the surface of the ground, was set with tiles showing some signs of wear. What manner of structure would have required so substantial a foundation it is difficult to say, but it can hardly have been a garden ornament. It is more likely to have supported a domestic feature,

The third century

73 Roman well in the southern courtyard of the East Wing. After the removal of part of the filling and the packing of the well pit the timber lining can clearly be seen

perhaps the base for a hand mill or even a press of some kind. If so, then the old garden had become part of the working area. There is certainly a logic behind these late modifications.

Nothing has yet been said of the fate of the West Wing during the second and third centuries largely because, while alterations to the original structure can be recognized, they cannot be dated. Within the rooms of the wing the observable changes were slight. The awkwardly shaped room W3 was divided by a wall laid directly on the original mosaic (thus incidentally preserving a wide strip from later destruction) and in room W6, immediately to the south, the worn mosaic floor was patched with red *tesserae* while some form of projecting plinth was built out from the wall. These are the only surviving alterations, but the Saxon and medieval ploughing would have carried away all trace of any superficial late partition walls.

In the old East Wing the bath suite continued to function with no major alteration or refitting throughout the third century, but the easternmost wall of the building had been demolished to its footings and in all probability the roofs of the east range had long since been removed. There is no trace of any form of occupation, rebuilding or reflooring within the rooms after the Flavian period, with the exception of the small late hearth in room E2. Apart from this the only structure of post-Flavian date to survive, other than the baths, is a timber-lined well dug close to the north wall of the entrance hall in the south-east corner of the small courtyard (**73**). Some time during the late second or early third century it was abandoned and filled with rubbish of various kinds including pottery, part of a basin of Purbeck marble and a large section of a base belonging to a column. The siting of the well is particularly interesting because it was dug exactly over the bed of the old stream filled in in the 60s of the first century. Either its course had been divined or, more likely, the subsidence of the surrounding structures indicated the former water course, always supposing that the siting was not purely accidental.

Whatever happened to the southern part of the palace in the second and third centuries, it is clear that the entrance hall continued to stand for most of the time, although the marble lining from the pool would have been one of the first things to be taken away. At an early stage the colonnaded fronts to the hall were removed and excavation has shown how the gravel of the street gradually washed over the exposed footings right up to the front entrance, suggesting that vehicles as well as pedestrians now had access. Traffic through the hall was heavy and soon wore away the mortar floor. To begin with attempts were made to patch it but eventually they ceased allowing vehicle wear to cut deeply into the clay make-up beneath. After a while the volume of traffic lessened sufficiently to allow a layer of turf to form over the northern part of the hall, but pedestrians and carts still hugged the south wall. Then the roof fell in: the old rafters finally gave way and masses of tiles collapsed onto the floor. Complete tiles, if there were any left by this time, would have been carried away, leaving the rest of the fragments where they had fallen to be trampled under foot. The tiles show very clearly how the traffic funnelled between the piers of the western bay, wearing smooth the fragments lying in the main path but leaving those close against the walls and piers freshly broken and untrampled. Where all this traffic was going is not immediately apparent. It was evidently turning off the road into or across the area of the Flavian garden. If the South Wing had been demolished at an early date, a track might well have led down to the harbour, but positive evidence is lacking.

Towards the end of the century it is possible to detect signs that a new building programme was underway. In room N1 in the extreme north-west corner of the North Wing, work began on the construction of a new hypocaust system (**Col 26**). Instead of digging out the hypocaust chambers below the existing floor level, the new installations were constructed on the floor, the intention being to create a new level some 2–3ft above it. In the centre of the room the main hypocaust chamber, measuring about 8ft square, was constructed of a floor of upturned roof tiles with side walls built of greensand blocks and bonding courses of tiles set in clay. On the floor were erected thirteen *pilae* composed of broken tiles which were to support the raised floor. Into the north side of the chamber opened the hot air inlet, a wide channel covered with overlapping roof tiles. The recurring use of roof tiles, which were probably expensive to produce and were certainly unsuitable for the purpose of general building, is interesting. It suggests that the builders had at their disposal a quantity of second-hand tiles, salvaged perhaps from some other part of the building, and used these rather than going to the expense of buying new bricks. The corners of the chamber were joined by channels running diagonally to the corners of the room where they would have met vertical vents set in the walls. This kind of arrangement would have worked very efficiently for the hot air from the stokery would have been drawn through the system by the updraught created by the chimneys. As soon as the required temperature was reached stoking would have ceased, the room remaining hot for a considerable time by virtue of the heat absorbed by the surrounding masonry. This kind of Roman hypocaust embodies the same principles as modern night-storage heaters.

This was the kind of system which the builders had intended to insert into the room. They had got as far as constructing the foundation works and had begun to fill in the spaces between the channels with rubble when building ceased. Two pieces of evidence allow this conclusion to be reached: first, a careful examination of the mouth of the flue showed that the tiles and the clay in which they had been set bore no discoloration as they would have done had they been subjected to heat, nor was there any ash or charcoal in the channel. Second, there was no trace of a broken-up floor in the chamber beneath the centre of the room. The conclusion must be that the system was never fired and that in all probability the floor had never been laid.

Some further light was thrown on the situation by the discovery, in room N3 to the south, of two large heaps of a coarse gritty mortar mixed up ready for use and actually retained by planks to prevent spreading. This may have been the mortar intended for the floor above the hypocaust.

There are other signs of building activity in progress at this time. In the West Wing the mosaic in room W3 was being uprooted. *Tesserae* had been shovelled into heaps in the corner of the room where they still lay 1600 years later, but many sack-loads must have been carried off, perhaps for temporary storage in the old aisled hall where a large heap of loose stones was found. They may have been intended as raw material waiting for the mosaicist who was to lay a new floor above the hypocaust. Finally, in room N11, a substantial heap of window panes had been amassed; they were stacked on the floor in the corner of the room ready to be used again when the reconstruction had reached a sufficiently advanced stage.

Other minor works were undertaken at this time or a little earlier; the partition wall across the passage between rooms N1 and 3 had been removed, facilitating movement between the two rooms, which might have helped the efficiency of the building programme. The partition between the two rooms of the kitchen, built into the east veranda of the corridor, was also pulled down. Both compartments were then refloored together and a new oven, showing little sign of use, was built.

There are, then, clear signs that building work was in progress towards the end of the third century. What was in the minds of the owners it is impossible now to say, but one room was being fitted out with an expensive system of under-floor heating and it may be that more extensive alterations were about to be undertaken, using up stockpiles of tesserae, window panes, roof tiles and probably timbers derived from the demolition of now defunct pieces of the old building. After all, the building was 200 years old, and had not been updated for at least 80 years. It is no wonder that a little modernization was being carried out. In the Province generally the late third and early fourth century was a time of extensive building programmes, particularly in the countryside. It was now that the great country mansions were beginning to reach their most developed form. Indeed there was sufficient work available for schools of mosaicists to become established in many of the main urban centres. Perhaps the owners of Fishbourne had set in train a scheme of renovation to bring the old villa up to date, but their plans were never to be realized.

11. Fire and destruction

Some time, towards the end of the third century, the inhabited part of the North Wing was enveloped by a disastrous fire which completely destroyed the superstructure of the building, leaving it a gutted ruin. The evidence is dramatic. Everywhere over the floors lay a thick blanket of broken and discoloured roof tiles, rafter nails and charred roof timbers, in some places up to a foot thick. The roof was ablaze long enough for the lead fittings to melt and drip onto the mosaics, forming large puddles of the molten metal; then, with the rafters weakened by the flames, the roof collapsed, some of the debris falling into the molten lead. The timbers continued to burn, discolouring the mosaics and tessellated floors with streaks of grey and blue, the heat being intense enough to refire the tiles from which the tesserae were made and occasionally to vitrify fragments of the roof tiles.

Inside, the doors, door sills and timber partitions went up in flames. Several of the completely charred door sills still remain in position as witness to the fact and when the corridor in front of room N7 was being excavated traces of its large doors were found where they had fallen forward. All that now remained were the iron strap hinges with the nails by which they were attached still in position, lying amidst the charcoal. In room N11 the falling roof smashed the stacks of window panes and in places the heat was so intense that the glass melted and the panes buckled and contorted. One of them, which had been lying on an oyster, was so softened by the heat that it took up the shape of the shell.

The southern part of room N12 was, at the time of the fire, used as a store room. Somewhere on its south wall was a shelf upon which had been placed a wooden box or tray, with its angles strengthened with iron bindings, a number of pots of normal kitchen ware and one large storage vessel containing a variety of lentils. The whole lot was completely smashed by the falling roof, the individual sherds breaking apart and being refired by the heat from the burning rafters, so that when the pots were stuck together normal black and grey coloured fragments joined to bright red pieces which had become oxidized in the flames.

All kinds of objects must have been lying about the building at the time, but only a few remained to be discovered. In the northern half of room N12 a group of iron fittings had been left about, including a length of chain, a padlock and three iron hipposandals (a kind of horse-shoe). In room N3 the remains of an axle were found, all that now survived being the iron axle-caps and the iron linchpins which kept the wheels in position. There must have been innumerable other fittings and items of furniture, no trace of which survived the blaze.

Immediately the flames had died down, people returned to the burnt out ruin. All the walls, with the exception of the one between rooms N3 and 4, were still standing, many of them with their discoloured wall plaster still in position, but the roof must have completely gone and the floors were obscured beneath heaps of charred debris. Then the task of salvaging began. People raked carefully through the rubble taking away anything of value, including any complete roof tiles that may have survived. This much is clear from the nature of the rubble itself. The charred rafters had been churned up, and the roof tiles turned over so that fragments discoloured in an oxidizing atmosphere were lying immediately next to those discoloured under reducing conditions. This could only have happened after the fire had died down. The salvaging was thorough for not a single complete roof tile remained.

One of the issues to arise is how far the fire spread. As we shall see, the detached East Wing baths were not affected but the flames could easily have spread to the West Wing. Saxon and medieval ploughing had removed most of the rubble but in those places where some rubble does survive, in the apse of the audience chamber and the basement of the hypocaust chamber, there was no trace of burning. On the other hand areas of discoloration appear on the mosaic in room W8, a burnt door sill survives between rooms W7 and 9, and the painted plaster from the corridor behind the audience chamber has been badly scorched. On balance, then, it seems that the West Wing probably suffered burning. The absence of roof nails is, however, puzzling, unless we suppose that part of the roof had been demolished or was being demolished in connection with the general rebuilding.

The baths in the East Wing escaped the flames because of their isolated position, but a bath building with no attached house was of very little value and the decision seems to have been taken to demolish it. First of all the suspended floors of the hypocaust were smashed up so that the useful *pilae* tiles and box tiles could be reached and the tiles, particularly the square ones of which the *pilae* were built, were systematically removed while the rubble and ash was shovelled out into neighbouring rooms. At this stage no attempt was made to dismantle the walls; it was the tiles which the salvagers were after. The date at which the fire occurred can be defined within certain limits from the archaeological evidence. The pottery smashed by the collapse of the roof includes a number of coarseware types currently in use in the middle and latter part of the third century, while the finer wares are of types normally found in the late third and early fourth century. On this evidence a late third-century date is indicated. Even greater precision is provided by the group of 43 coins from the rubbish thrown out of the baths at the time of the demolition. All belong to the period 270–96, the common issues of the early fourth century being completely absent. This would suggest that the post-fire demolition of the baths probably took place at the very end of the 290s.

The burning of the building occurred in a turbulent period of British history. From the mid 280s Britain had been ruled as a breakaway state by the usurper Carausius, a marine who had originally been given the task of driving off the pirates then marauding along the Channel coasts. His enemies in Rome had accused him of being in league with the pirates, by allowing them to land and pillage the coastal regions and then sharing their booty. This may have been so — at any event a return to Rome would probably have meant death. Carausius decided to make a stand, taking Britain as his empire together with part of the Gaulish coast, centred on Boulogne. Although the Gaulish territory was soon lost, Carausius maintained his British empire and appears to have made many reforms, particularly to the coinage which was restored to a more stable basis, and there is some evidence of increasing prosperity in the towns and countryside. It was possibly in this new spirit that the rebuilding began at Fishbourne.

The murder of Carausius by his close supporter Allectus in 293 marked the beginning of growing unrest. Three years later, as the result of a carefully planned attack, the central Roman authorities led by Constantius Chlorus finally overran the breakaway province and restored it to the empire. The attack was a dramatic reminder of the vital importance of sea power to the defence of Britain. Constantius had divided his force into two: one arm, sailing west, outflanked the British fleet in the Channel and landed somewhere on the south coast. Marching inland they encountered Allectus and his army and soundly beat them. The other arm sailed along the Thames and arrived in London in time to stop the remnants of the beaten force from sacking the town. Britain was now safely restored to the Roman empire — an event recorded on the reverse of a famous gold medallion from Arras.

All this was happening whilst the final drama was being played out at Fishbourne. Some link between local and national events is not impossible. Undefended buildings close to the south coast would have been in some danger throughout much of the last thirty years of the century, but we cannot with any certainty assign the destruction of Fishbourne to the major events of recorded history. The fire could just as well have been caused by a careless workman as by the invading army of Constantius.

The return of Britain to Roman rule marked the beginning of a period of considerable prosperity. It was now that the villas began to reach their maximum size with all the luxuries of bath suites, central heating and elaborate mosaics. In the towns, too, there is evidence of widespread rebuilding. But at Fishbourne nothing remained except a fire-scarred ruin.

Why the villa was not rebuilt after the fire we can only guess. The masonry superstructure cannot have been badly damaged; minor repairs to the walls, complete reroofing and a replastering and painting would have restored the building quite adequately. But this was not done — instead the walls were systematically dismantled. It could be that the natural environment was becoming hostile. We know that throughout the third century coastal regions of Britain were experiencing severe flooding as the result of a rise in mean sea-level. The marsh was certainly encroaching on Fishbourne. By this stage much of the southern garden was permanently waterlogged, while to the north of the palace spring water continued to be dammed up and marshy conditions were spreading over the made-up area which had previously been dry land. There was no simple solution to the problem, even large-scale drainage works would not have counteracted the flooding. While it is true that the marsh did not encroach upon the built-up area itself, the proximity of insect-infested swamps can hardly have been conducive to comfortable living. It is not difficult to visualize that day, towards the end of the third century, when the owner stood on the site and, looking from the burnt-out building to the encroaching marsh, finally made the decision to move elsewhere.

Fire and destruction

74 The opening of the palace was preceded by a programme of conservation. Floors were consolidated and fallen wall plaster was replaced in its original position

Fire and destruction

This did not mean the cessation of activity on the site. Far from it. The ruins were an extremely valuable source of building stone, particularly for the growing town of Chichester only a mile away. The fine ashlar masonry of the walls, the stylobate blocks and gutters and the columns would all have had a cash value particularly in an area like this where good building stone is hard to come by.

For some time after the fire the ruins were left standing, and under the effects of weathering plaster began to peel off the walls and accumulate in heaps, over the burnt debris of the roof. In a few years the depth of material amounted to $2-2\frac{1}{2}$ ft. It was only after this period of neglect that robbing began and the walls were systematically demolished down to the flint cobble footings, which often lay 1-2ft below the floor levels. The rubble left over after the usable building stone had been recovered was thrown back into the trenches and piled up in the rooms. The robbing was very precise below ground level and quite often the wall plaster, against the face of which the collapsed rubble had piled up, was left in a vertical position after the stone of the wall had been removed. The plaster facing the west wall of room N1, for example, still remained in its original position, kept in place by the collapsed material inside the room and the thrown-back rubble in the robber trench behind. The robbing of the west wall of room N12 produced slightly different results. Here the painted plaster on both faces remained standing to a height of 2ft whilst the wall was being robbed, but before the robber trench could be filled the plaster collapsed, first the west face and then the east. When this area was excavated it was possible to remove both layers of fallen plaster one after the other and to restore a section of them to their original positions (**74**).

An examination of the walls of the North Wing shows that, while most of them have been robbed to the flint footings, some sections survived. Usually there is an explanation for this. In the case of the east end of the wing the walls had been demolished to ground level during the second century and nothing showed above ground by the time of the early fourth-century robbing to indicate the positions of the worthwhile remaining stone. The wall between rooms N3 and 4 still survived to a height of about 2ft, but this was because the wall had collapsed during the fire and nothing remained above the general rubble level to give the stone robbers any idea that masonry survived just below. At the west end of the wing the stone beneath the door sills usually remained untouched. After all, to get at it would have meant removing an overburden of 2–3ft of rubble from the doorways and this was not considered to be worthwhile. Nor, apparently, was it considered to be worth the effort of removing up to 4ft of collapsed building to reach the stylobate blocks and gutters buried deep in the north-west corner of the garden. Where the rubble cover was shallow however, away from the corner, everything was taken.

The stones of the wall and the large stylobate blocks would have been reusable in their original form but the gutter blocks were an awkward shape. Along the north side of the East Wing courtyard the individual slabs had been dragged out of position and the flanges knocked off and discarded before the rest of the block was carried away.

Systematic demolition on this scale must have taken a number of people some time to complete; many hundreds of tons of stone had to be loosened, cleaned, stacked, loaded and carted off. It seems that those engaged on the work probably camped for a while in the shell of the old East Wing, while the demolition of the North and West Wings was in progress. During this time a layer of occupation rubbish 6–9in thick accumulated on the floor of rooms E1–3, overlying the destroyed footings of the apse belonging to the *tepidarium*. It may be that the two hearths in room E2 belonged to this date, representing perhaps the place where the demolition gang ate and lived for the duration of the job. The pottery from that layer is the latest Roman ware to be found on the site, difficult to date with precision but assignable to the early fourth century — a date which fits well with the period during which the robbing is thought to have taken place. A few late coins dating to the first 20 years or so of the fourth century have been found scattered about the site, but they are very few indeed compared with the late third-century issues. Clearly by now occupation was at an end and when eventually, between AD 310–20, the last load of stone was removed and the demolition gang packed up and departed, they left behind them weed-covered heaps of rubble, with the old palace garden long since overgrown and gone wild, and on both sides a gradually encroaching swamp. After 250 years of intensive occupation on a grand scale, nature was again taking over.

12. Aftermath

While Chichester flourished in the fourth century, Fishbourne passed from memory beneath a thickening mantle of soil, the weather, worms, and plant growth combining to level out the contours of the now grass-grown mounds of debris. At some later date in the sub-Roman or early Saxon period the site was used as a cemetery, for a group of at least four burials had been laid in graves cut down into the rubble of the old building (75). The absence of coffin nails or shroud pins leaves us ignorant as to the exact manner of burial but three of the bodies were laid on their backs in an extended position with hands neatly folded over the pelvis in a manner clearly indicating careful burial. The fourth also lay on his back, but with knees flexed. Since three of the burials were orientated north–south, they are unlikely to be Christians and therefore some date in the immediate post-Roman period seems likely. More than this, it is impossible to say.

The burials, like most of the rest of the site, were covered with a layer of grey soil containing finely broken-up mortar and rubble, representing ploughsoil created by long years of agricultural activity. Its thickness varied considerably from one part of the site to another, from a few inches over the West Wing to more than 3ft thick immediately in front of it. Over the rather more level ground of the East Wing it averaged 18in. From this ploughsoil came abraded potsherds ranging in date from the late Saxon period down to the sixteenth or seventeenth century with the characteristic green-glazed sherds of thirteenth- or fourteenth-century pitchers being the most common. The pottery must have come from kitchen and household refuse spread on the fields as manure derived from the houses of the medieval village of Fishbourne that was growing up on the promontory of land between the two inlets on either side of Mill Lane which leads down to the harbour. This area has produced a number of larger sherds of medieval pottery from the Mill Pond and also from the gardens of the modern houses. The site of the Roman palace had thus become the fields of a medieval peasant village.

Several coins of medieval and later date were found in the ploughsoil, including a silver penny of Henry II or III, a groat of Henry VI and a half-groat of Henry VII or VIII. These too were probably brought out from the village in cart-loads of manure.

The limits of three medieval strip fields were identified during the excavation. They had cut into the Roman floors of the West Wing, removing even the floor make-up in some areas, and leaving the edges of the ploughed areas sharply defined. It was because of this ploughing that so much of the West Wing was destroyed. The 15ft wide baulks

Aftermath

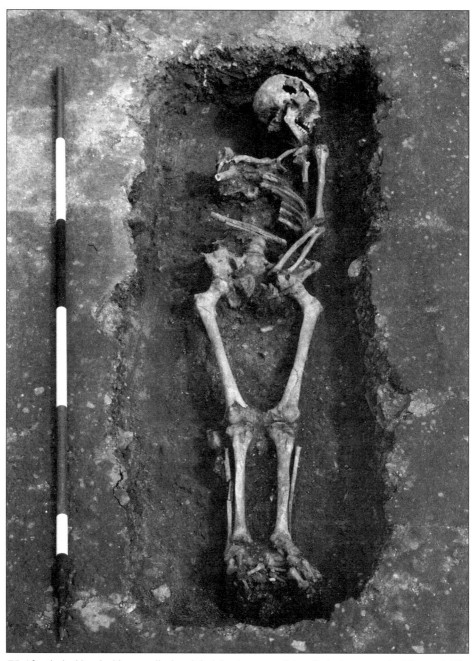

75 *After the building had been totally demolished the site was used, in a limited way, as a burial ground. The exact date of the interments is unknown, but they may well be of the fifth century*

between the fields, which were left unploughed, have allowed strips of the original floors to survive and even larger areas remained intact beneath the headlands where the plough turned round at the end of each strip.

The strips were about 68ft wide and probably a little over 400ft long. No traces of continuous boundaries have been found between them, but a length of ditch marks the south side of one field and a ditch and three large pits were found in the baulk on the north side of another. The ditches probably result from attempts at draining particularly wet areas, while the pits might have been caused by tree growth along the boundary. The three fields cover much of the excavated areas, making it difficult to define the limits of agriculture, but fields may well have continued to the north up to the swampy area and at least one more field would have existed between the southernmost now recognizable and the line of the road. On the south side of the road some trace of medieval ploughing can be recognized but the proximity of the saltwater marsh would not have allowed width for more than a single strip.

While the West Wing was being ploughed the medieval farmers could hardly have failed to notice the flint footings of the Roman walls which would have caught the ploughshare in a tiresome manner. Thus when flint was needed for building in the village the old ruin served to provide it. Several of the footings in the West Wing were completely removed at this time, as sherds of medieval pottery in the robber trenches show. Even one of the much deeper East Wing footings was robbed out for its flints. So deep was the robbing in all these cases that it can hardly have been simply to remove an obstruction to the plough. Indeed the ploughs were dragged through most of the intransigent soils, as the plough furrows gouged through the clay of the garden and the mosaic in room N13 show.

It is probable that the ploughing continued unabated until the time of the Enclosures in the eighteenth century, when the new larger fields were laid out with deep V-shaped ditches and thorn hedges — the boundaries which were still in existence when excavations began in 1961. The new fields followed very closely the boundaries and alignments of those which they enclosed. It was during the eighteenth century that the village began to spread from its nucleus out along the south side of the road and eventually to the north side to where the house now known as 'The Bays' was built, together with its stable and yard which now cover the northern part of the proto-palace.

The nineteenth century saw the cessation of ploughing, allowing a rich stone-free topsoil to form which, some time towards the middle of the century, was disturbed by a system of land drainage constructed over the somewhat clayey area which had once been the formal Roman garden (Col 14). Only a single pond was left towards the centre. It continued in use but was filled in when piped water was laid to water troughs. When it was re-excavated in 1966, in connection with the examination of the Roman garden, the hoof marks of the last few cows who drank from it in the summer of 1938 could still be recognized.

By 1960 the village had grown considerably, spreading out in all directions from its old nucleus, and it was only the discovery and subsequent purchase of the site of the palace that prevented it, too, from being engulfed by modern housing development and becoming a suburb of Chichester.

Glossary

apodyterium	an undressing room	**hypocaust**	a system of underfloor heating using hot air
apse	semicircular recess in a wall or room	*imbrex*	a curved roof tile covering the joins between adjacent flat tiles (*tegulae*)
architrave	horizontal member immediately above a row of columns		
basilica	an aisled hall with roof supported on pairs of piers	**lunette**	curve-topped opening often in the end of a vaulted roof
bead-and-reel	decorative moulding incorporating repetitive motifs	*opus sectile*	coloured stone cut into geometric shapes arranged in patterns
caldarium	the hot room in a bathing establishment	**pediment**	the triangular gable end of a temple above the front columns
colonnade	row of columns		
cornice	uppermost member of the entablature	**peristyle**	a colonnaded walk arranged around an open area
egg-and-dart	decorative moulding incorporating repetitive motifs	*pilae*	square tiles set one upon another to form pillars to support the floors of hypocausts
entablature	the horizontal members (architrave, frieze and cornice) above a row of columns	**portico**	porch area
		revetting	a structure, usually a wall, used to retain soil when levels change
frieze	part of the entablature (between the architrave and cornice) above a row of columns	**stylobate**	stone foundation blocks for a colonnade
		tegulae	flat roof tiles with upturned flanges
frigidarium	cold room in a bathing establishment	*tepidarium*	the warm room in a bath suite
guilloche	a braided or twisted motif common in mosaics	**voussoir**	wedge-shaped brick or stone used in constructing arches

Visiting the Site

The Roman palace at Fishbourne now belongs to the Sussex Archaeological Society. It is open to the public at the following times:

mid-February to mid-December – daily from 10am, closing 4–6pm depending on the time of year.

mid-December to mid-February – Sundays only 10am–4pm.

For further information contact Fishbourne Roman Palace, Salthill Road, Fishbourne, Chichester, Sussex PO19 3QR. Tel: 01243 785859 Fax: 01243 539266.

Further reading

Antiquarian accounts of discoveries at Fishbourne
Gentleman's Magazine 1805 (ii), 926-7
Hampshire Telegraph and Sussex Chronicle Monday, 17 April 1806, p. 2, col. 3
T.W. Horsfield, *The History, Antiquities and Topography of the County of Sussex* (Lewes: 1835), Vol 2, 52
The Times 11 February 1929 (letters to editor)

The excavation reports
The main excavation which took place between 1961 and 1968 is published in full in two volumes:
> Barry Cunliffe, *Excavations at Fishbourne. Vol. I: The Site* and *Vol. II: The Finds* (Society of Antiquaries, London: 1971)

The excavations carried out at various times between 1969 and 1988 are fully reported in:
> Barry Cunliffe, Alec Down and David Rudkin, *Excavation at Fishbourne 1969–1988* (*Chichester Excavations* 9, Chichester: 1996)
> David Rudkin, Recent discoveries at Fishbourne Roman Palace [the early mosaic in room N7] . *Mosaic* 4 (1981), 8–10
> David Rudkin, Fishbourne Roman Palace: beneath the Medusa Mosaic *The Archaeology of Chichester and District* (1989), 27–9
> David Rudkin, Excavation at the Roman Palace, Fishbourne, 1983 *Sussex Archaeological Collections* 123 (1985), 256–9

Of the more recent work from 1992 onwards interim notes have appeared in the regular editions of *The Archaeology of Chichester and District* published by Southern Archaeology and *Sussex Past and Present*, the newsletter of the Sussex Archaeological Society.

General discussions

General discussions about Fishbourne and its chronology have appeared in various publications. Of particular significance are E.W. Black's papers:

>The dating of relief-patterned flue-tiles.
>>*Oxford Journal of Archaeology* 4 (1985), 353–76
>
>*The Roman Villas of south-east England* (BAR, Oxford: 1987).

Barry Cunliffe's reply:

>Fishbourne revisited: the site in its context.
>>*Journal of Roman Archaeology* 4 (1991), 160–9

and E.W. Black's comments on the proto-palace:

>The period 1C bath-building at Fishbourne and the problem of the 'proto-palace'. *Journal of Roman Archaeology* 6 (1993), 233–7

The career of Tiberius Claudius Togidubnus (Cogidubnus as he was conventionally known) has been frequently discussed. The most useful commentaries are:

>Peter Salway, *Roman Britain* (Oxford: 1981), 748–52
>
>A.A. Barrett, The career of Tiberius Claudius Cogidubnus.
>>*Britannia* 10 (1979), 227–42
>
>J.E. Bogaers, King Cogidubnus in Chichester. Another reading of *RIB* 91.
>>*Britannia* 10 (1979), 243–54.

The reason for adopting the spelling *Togidubnus* is given in:

>R.S.O. Tomlin, Reading a 1st-century Roman gold signet ring from Fishbourne. *Sussex Archaeological Collections* 135 (1997), 127–30.

Individual finds from Fishbourne

Most finds are discussed in the excavation reports but reports on items of special note include:

>M. Henig, A royal portrait head from Fishbourne, West Sussex.
>>*Journal of the British Archaeological Association* 149 (1996), 83–6
>
>R.S.O. Tomlin, Reading a 1st-century Roman gold signet ring from Fishbourne. *Sussex Archaeological Collections* 135 (1997), 127–30
>
>A. Down and M. Henig, A Roman *askos* handle from Fishbourne.
>>*Antiquaries Journal* 68 (1988), 308–10.

Roman Britain

There are many books on Roman Britain. Of these to be particularly recommended are:

>Sheppard Frere, *Britannia* (London: third edition 1987)
>
>Peter Salway, *Roman Britain* (Oxford: 1981)

The interesting suggestion that the main invasion force landed in the Solent area in AD 43 is well argued in:

>J.G.F. Hind, The Invasion of Britain in AD 43 - an alternative strategy for Aulus Plautius *Britannia* 20 (1989), 1–22.

Index

Note: Bold page numbers refer to illustrations in the text. The Colour Plates appear as *Plate 1* etc.

Agricola, Roman governor, 105
aisled hall: East Wing (Flavian), 85–7, **85**, **86**, **88**; modifications, 111, 112–14, **112**
Allectus, 143
Angmering, Roman villa, 46, 105, 107
aqueduct, Flavian palace, 100, 103
Arminius, 22
Atrebates tribe, 19, 20; kingdom of, 21, 109
audience chamber *see* West Wing
Augustus, Emperor, 20
Aulus Plautius, 21

bakeries and bread ovens (Flavian palace), 103–4, 132
ballista bolt, 28
Bath, 105
baths: East Wing (second-century), 116, **117**, 119, **120**, 121–2, **121**; North Wing (second-century), 111–13, **112**; proto-palace (South Wing), 44–5, 81, 89; public (Chichester), 107
belt plate and buckles, 28
Bitterne, 31
Boudican rebellion, 109
Boulogne, 20, 21
bricks, from Dell Quay, 40
bridge, timber, 34, *Plate 2*

Britain: Carausius's rebellion, 142–3; pre-Roman, 19–20; Romanization of, 105, 107, *see also* Claudian invasion
buckles, 28

Camulodunum (Colchester), 21
Carausius, usurper, 142–3
Catuarus, Tiberius Claudius, 108
Catuvellauni tribe, 19, 20, 21
cemeteries, post-Roman, 31, 147, **148**
Cherusci tribe (Germany), 22
Chichester: Iron Age entrenchments, 17–18; military fort at, 31; Roman town, 22, 38, 107, 145, 147; Temple of Neptune and Minerva, 22
Chichester Civic Society, 9, 13
Chichester Inlet, 17, 25, **26**, *see also* harbour
Cirencester, 105
Claudian invasion (AD 43), 21, 29, 31; possible landings at Fishbourne, 21, 31
Claudius, Emperor, 20, 22
clay pits, Dell Quay, 40
coastal erosion, 18
coastal flooding, 143
Cogidubnus *see* Togidubnus
coins: Claudian, 28; fourth century, 146; Hadrian, 116; in Iron Age economy, 17, 18, 19; medieval, 147; Septimius Severus, 135; third century, 142; Vespasian, 49
colonnades: Flavian palace, 52, 91–3, **92**,

157

101, *Plate 18*; North Wing, 76, 78; third century alterations, 135–6; timber buildings, 36–7; West Wing, 53, 55–6
columns: Corinthian capitals, 43, **43**; Flavian palace, 52, 92–3, **95**
Commius, British ruler, 19
conservation techniques, 14–15, **144**
Constantius Chlorus, 143
copper alloy objects, military, 28–9, **30**
craftsmen: foreign, 43, 44, 46; local, 114–15; for proto-palace, 40

Dallaway, James, 11
Dell Quay, 21; clay pits, 40
Dio, Cassius, 19, 21
Dobunni tribe, 20, 23
Domitian: coins of, 49; Palace of, 57, 63, 87
Down, Alec, rescue excavations, 10, 104
drainage: from East Wing baths, 119, 121–2; from formal garden, 93, 95, 100
Dumnonii tribe, 31
Durotriges tribe, 20, 31

earthworks, Iron Age, 17–18
East Wing (Flavian palace), 13, 82–6, 89, 107; courtyard, **118**, **119**, 145; entrance hall, 82–5, **83**, **84**, 138; façade, 92; peristyle, 89; second-century baths, 116, **117**, 119, **120**, 121–2, **121**, 137; well, 137–8, **137**, *see also* aisled hall
Eastbourne, Roman villa, 107
Eccles (Kent), Roman villa, 105
economy, late Iron Age, 17, 19
entrance hall *see* East Wing
Epillus, British leader, 19
excavations, 9, 13–15; early finds, 11–13; gardens, 91; rescue, 10, 104; South Wing, 80–1
Exeter, 31

Fishbourne: harbour, 21, 31, 101; medieval village, 147, 149; roads, 33–4
Fosseway, 31
fountain (pool): in entrance hall, 83, 138; formal garden, 100–1

France, marble from, 40, 73, 74
furniture and fittings, evidence of, 76

Gaius, Emperor (Caligula), 20
garden (Neronian proto-palace), 41–2
gardens (Flavian palace), 14, 43, **93**, **94**, **97**, **99**, 149, *Plates 14–17*; bedding trenches, 91, 95–6, **96**, 97–9; informal south, 14, 101–3, **102**, 143; kitchen and herb, 103, 104; North Wing (private), 76, 78, 80, 101; plants, 95–6, 98–100; third century alterations, 136–7; water supply, 100–1, *see also* colonnades
glass, window, 139, 141
granaries, 26, **27**, 28

Hamworthy (Poole), 31
harbour, Roman, 12, 25, **26**, 29, 31, 33
Hayling Island, 105
helmet, legionary's bronze, 29
Herculaneum, 57, 74
hippodromos, West Wing, 63
Hod Hill (Dorset), 28, 31
Horsfield, T.W., 11
hypocaust: North Wing baths, 111, 135; North Wing (third century), 138–9, *Plate 26*; proto-palace, 45; West Wing (Flavian palace), 61

inscriptions: Temple of Neptune and Minerva, 22, 107; tribute to Nero, 33, 107
Iron Age, salt workings, 17
iron objects, 141–2
iron smithing, 40
Isle of Wight, 31

Julius Caesar, invasion, 20

kitchen garden (Flavian palace), 103, 132

latrines, East Wing, 122
Lepcis Magna, Hunting Baths, 45
Livia, Garden Room of (Prima Porta), 98
Lockleys, Roman farmhouse, 105
London, 105

Maiden Castle, 28
marble: Carrara, 40; from Turkey, 73, 74; imported, 40, 73–4; native (Purbeck), 40, 73, 74, 101
marble basin, 101
marble head, **106**, 108
marble wall inlay, 73
Margary, Ivan, 9
market garden (Flavian palace), 104
masonry, methods, 40
masonry buildings: in Flavian southern garden, 103; pre-Flavian (M1 and M3), 46–7
military buildings, 25–8, **29**, 31, 37, *Plate 1*, *see also* granaries; timber buildings
military equipment, finds, 28–9, **30**
mill (Flavian palace), 104
Mill pond, 13, 147
mosaic pavements, 14–15; audience chamber, 54–5; Cupid (Dolphin), 13, 14, 69, 124–5, **125–8**, 129, *Plates 19–21*; early finds, 11, 13; early third-century, 135, *Plate 25*; Medusa (North Wing), **113**, 113–14, **114**; North Wing, 65–6, **66–9**, 71, **71**, **73**, 74–5, **75–7**, 76, 78; Peacock, 130; polychrome, 58, 78, 124, 130; proto-palace, 44; second century, 15, 114–15, 123–32, *Plates 22–4*; West Wing, 57–9, **58–64**, 61–3, *see also opus sectile*
museum and cover building, 14, 15

Nero, Emperor, 33
North Wing (Flavian palace), 13–14, 64–5, **65**, **70**, 71, 80, *Plate 3*, *Plate 4*; corridor, 115, 123; demolition of eastern end, 115–16, 123, 145; mosaics, 65–6, **66–9**, 71, **71**, **73**, 74–5, **75–7**, 76, 78, *Plate 5*, *Plate 7*; new mosaics (second-century), 123–32, **124**, **125–8**; ruins robbed, 145; second-century alterations, 123–4, **131**; second-century bath suite, 111–13, 122; third century mosaics, 135, *Plate 25*; wall plaster, 70, 71–3, 75–6, 78, 80, *see also* working areas

opus sectile floors, proto-palace, 44, *Plate 12*
opus signinum flooring, 123

palace, Flavian: artificial terrace, 49–50, 91, 101–2; building materials, 50–2; design, **51**, 52–3; fire (third century), 141–2, 143; location, **50**; northern enclosure, 103–4; ownership, 108–9; ruins robbed for stone, 143, 145, 149; second-century alterations, 69, 111–16, 123–4, 130–3, **131**; third century alterations, 135–9, *see also* baths; East Wing; gardens; North Wing; South Wing; West Wing
Park Street, Roman farmhouse, 105
peristyles: East Wing (Flavian palace), 89; proto-palace, 89
Pliny the Elder: description of gardens, 97, 98, 99, 101; on mason's methods, 40
Pliny the Younger, 99
ploughing, Saxon and medieval, 54, 137, 142, 147, 149
Pompeii, 49, 57
pond: Flavian southern garden, 102, *see also* fountain
Poole Harbour, 19, 31
pottery: imported samian ware, 28, 49; Iron Age, 17; late, 146; medieval, 147; used in mosaics, 115, 129
proto-palace (Neronian), 39–40, 41, **41**, **42**, 107; baths, 44–5, 81, 89; garden, 41–2; incorporated in Flavian South Wing, 45, 81
Pulborough, Roman villa, 46, 107

Regnenses people (Chichester), 22
Richborough, *mansio*, 87
rings, finger, 108
roads, 31–2; Fishbourne, 33–4
Rudkin, David, Curator, 9

salt extraction, 17
Selsey: decline of, 33; harbour, 19; Iron Age settlement, 18, 22

159

servants' quarters, 46, 104
Shaw, Rev. N., 11
Silchester, *mansio*, 87
South Wing (Flavian palace), 14, 80–1, 107; informal garden, 14, 101–3, **102**, 143; Neronian baths incorporated in, 45, 81
Southwick, Roman villa, 46, 107
Stabiae, wall painting, 80
Stane Street, 21, 33
statuary: garden, 96; marble head, **106**, 108
stone: Bembridge limestone, 52; Caen, 52; greensand, 51; Mixon limestone, 51–2; oolitic limestone, 52; types, 40; Wealden siltstone, 40
stone ballast, 37–8
stream, 34–5, **34**, 39, 93, 138
stucco: Flavian palace, 56–7, 69–70, **72**, *Plate 8*; proto-palace, 44
stylobates: Flavian palace, 52, 81, 92, 145; proto-palace, 42–3
subsidence, North Wing, 116
Sussex Archaeological Society, 9, 10
Sussex Archaeological Trust, 13, 14

Tacitus, 21–2, 105, 108–9
Temple of Neptune and Minerva (Chichester), 22
terrace, artificial, 49–50, 91, 101–2
tiles, roof, 40; reused roof, 138; salvaged after fire, 142; *tegulae*, 52
timber, 52; oak piles, 51
timber buildings, 13, 25–6; demolished, 39, 107; granaries, 26, **27**, 28; Neronian, 34–7, **34**, **35**, **36**, *see also* masonry buildings; military buildings
Tincomarus, British ruler, 19
Titus, Emperor, 107
Togidubnus, Tiberius Claudius, 21–3, 31, 107; inscription, 107, **108**; as likely owner of Fishbourne, 108–9
trade, with Rome, 19
Turkey, marble from, 73, 74

Verica, Atrebatic leader, 19–21, 22

Verulamium, 37, 105, 130
Vespasian, 21, 31; as emperor, 49, 109

Waddon Hill, 31
wall plaster, painted, **144**, 145, *Plate 10*; colonnades, 76, 78, 92; East Wing baths, 121; external West Wing, 97; mock marbling, 59, 64, 76, 129–30; North Wing (Flavian palace), 70, 71–3, 75–6, 78, 80; proto-palace, 44, *Plate 9*; West Wing (Flavian palace), 59, 61, 62, 63–4
water supply: aqueduct, 100, 103; North Wing baths, 112–13; southern garden, 102; tank, 100, 132; to formal garden, 100–1
Watling Street, 21
well, East Wing (Flavian palace), 137–8, **137**
West Wing (Flavian palace), 14, 53–4, **53**, 64, 107–8, *Plate 13*; audience chamber, 54–7, **54**, **55**, **56**, **57**, 64; corridor, 63–4; later alterations, 137; later ploughing over, 54, 137, 142, 147, 149; mosaics, 57–9, **58–64**, 61–3, 139, *Plate 6*; wall plaster, 59, 61, 62, 63–4
Weymouth, 31
Wiggonholt, Roman villa, 46
window glass, 139, 141
Woodchester, Roman villa, 105
working areas: for Flavian palace, 103–4, 113, 132; for proto-palace, 39–40; timber buildings, 36; within formal garden (third century), 136–7